Saddleback Sightseeing In California

A Guide To Rental Horses, Trail Rides And Guest Ranches

By John A. Greenwald

GEM GUIDES BOOK CO.
315 Cloverleaf Dr., Suite F
Baldwin Park, CA 91706

Cover photograph, McGee Canyon, by Londie G. Padelsky.

Photograph of author by Carol Greenwald.

All other photographs by author.

Cover design by Steve Laurie

Library of Congress Catalogue Number 92-53796
ISBN 0-935182-58-6

To my wife, Carol, whose enthusiastic encouragement and unwavering support made it all possible.

TABLE OF CONTENTS

INTRODUCTION

There are those who will argue that the growing interest in horseback riding in California was primarily stimulated by movies like *City Slickers* and the Academy Award-winning *Dances With Wolves*. Others will suggest that it was the enormous popularity of the epic book and miniseries *Lonesome Dove* that gave this activity a boost.

All have had an impact, of course. But the truth of the matter is that the popularity of horseback riding has been growing for years. Call it nostalgia or a high-touch response to our high-tech times. But, whatever the explanation, more people than ever are discovering the joys of riding tall in the saddle.

The only reason that even more people aren't going on trail rides and cattle drives, or visiting guest ranches, is that there's been a lack of information about all that is available.

Saddleback Sightseeing in California, a comprehensive guide listing over 80 rental stables, pack stations, and guest ranches, was written to correct this problem. Included are listings from every geographical area in California, covering activities for all ability levels, ages, and needs.

Detailed descriptions of the individual rides have been provided, so that you'll know what to expect before you climb into the saddle. You can compare rides, rates, even outfitters.

In preparing this guide, every effort has been made to provide fair, objective information about each location, allowing you to be an informed consumer. All the places listed in *Saddleback Sightseeing in California* have something worthwhile to offer. That's not to say, however, that every place will satisfy everyone's needs. But, with the information provided, you should be able to make educated decisions about the services that will best satisfy your needs.

Rates for all activities have been included, because it's impossible to accurately evaluate an activity, if you don't know how much it costs. There is, however, one caveat. The rates, though current at press time, are subject to change. Therefore, it's always a good idea to call in advance to confirm the rates before you decide to go riding.

To assist you as you read the book, an explanation of certain terminology might be helpful. The term lope, for instance, has been used throughout the book. For those unfamiliar with the term, it's the word western-style riders use to mean canter.

Certain pack station terminology has been used as well. The term spot trip describes a pack trip on which you ride with a wrangler and pack animals to a predetermined destination and are left at that spot. The wrangler returns at the end of your stay and you ride out together.

An extended trip is one on which the wrangler remains with you during the entire outing. You're required to do your own cooking and camp chores, however. An all inclusive trip is similar to an extended trip, except that all meals are provided and the wranglers do most of the camp chores. In addition, pack stations also offer dunnage services, meaning they'll pack in food and gear for hikers. However, since this is a riding book, not a hiking book, dunnage services are not mentioned.

For those interested in a guest ranch experience, be sure to read the descriptions carefully, because the ranches differ greatly one from another. Some are quite modern. Others are extremely rustic. Many offer non-stop activities, while a few provide the wonderful option of doing absolutely nothing. After reviewing all of them, you are sure to find a ranch that's just right for you.

As for the hourly trail rides, the rule is, the longer the ride the better the scenery. That is not a hard and fast rule, however, and the book notes some important exceptions. But, generally, the shorter rides have less to offer. Unfortunately, the shorter rides are the ones most people tend to select. Hopefully, this book will encourage you at least to try the longer, more scenic rides.

Regardless of which rides you select, however, the important thing is to enjoy yourself. If this book helps you get out from behind your desk and away from the freeway snarl for even a few hours of good, old-fashioned fun, then it has more than succeeded. Let me know how it goes. If you have any comments about the book or your own riding experiences, please write to me at P.O. Box 4233, Irvine, California 92716. In the meantime, happy trails to you.

Feeding time at Coffee Creek Ranch

NORTH COAST AND MOUNTAINS 1

COFFEE CREEK RANCH

HC 2, Box 4940
Trinity Center, CA 96091-9502
(916) 266-3343
Owners: Ruth and Mark Hartman

With peaks barely exceeding 9,000 feet and land area amounting to only 525,000 acres, the Trinity Alps might seem relatively insignificant in a state that boasts the Sierra Nevada. But what they lack in size, the Alps more than make up for in scenic beauty. Picture-postcard views abound in this region of snowcapped mountains, cascading waterfalls, lush meadows, and sparkling lakes.

In the heart of it all is the Coffee Creek Ranch. Sitting at 3,100 feet in elevation, near Trinity Center, the 127-acre ranch offers guests one of the best ways available to enjoy the unique Trinity Alps scenery. So well regarded is the program at Coffee Creek Ranch, that it has twice earned Honorable Mention in *Family Circle* magazine's "Resort of the Year" awards.

With a history as colorful as the country that surrounds it – the property was lost twice in poker games at the turn of the century and was a source for bootleg liquor during Prohibition – Coffee Creek Ranch provides a full range of interesting activities for guests all year round.

The most popular activity, of course, is horseback riding, available from April through October each year. Those participating are divided according to ability level, with experienced riders grouped separately. Riders wishing to lope or gallop may do so by special arrangement.

Typically, two rides are scheduled each day. Three mornings a week– Sunday, Tuesday, and Thursday – guests can go on breakfast rides to a creek-side spot called Onion Flat, where a delicious, hot breakfast awaits them. There is also a picnic ride on Monday mornings to the Wagner Mine, a gold mine up behind the ranch. Guests get to examine an old rock crusher before sitting down to their picnic lunch. On alternative picnic rides, guests visit nearby Benson Gulch, home to the California pitcher plant (*Darlingtonia californica*), which like the venus fly trap eats flies. Kids, in particular, get a kick out of this.

The ranch schedules a twilight ride on Monday afternoons and a swim ride on Tuesday afternoons. On the twilight trip, riders follow Boulder Creek Road up to the top of a hill. This is one place where experienced riders can even gallop. Everyone else must walk. Once on top, riders have a splendid view looking out over Coffee Creek Canyon as the sun sets. For the swim ride, guests travel to a natural swimming hole in Boulder Creek, where they're able to swim right under a 25-foot high waterfall.

The most interesting rides of the week, however, are the all-day trips scheduled on Wednesdays. Following Boulder Creek, riders climb past the waterfall all the way to Lion Lake. Sitting in a glacier-sculpted, granite bowl, at 7,000 feet in elevation, the deep, heart-shaped lake provides an excellent photo opportunity. It's also a great spot for fishing, swimming, and hiking.

After enjoying Lion Lake and its surroundings, and eating lunch, the riders continue on to Sugar Pine Lake, a larger, deeper body of water sitting at a slightly lower elevation. High rock walls, jagged at the top, surround it, while trees cluster along the shoreline. Ironically, only a few of the trees are sugar pine. Guests explore the area around the lake and then follow Sugar Pine Creek back down to Coffee Creek Road.

Guests interested in the history of the region might prefer the alternative all-day trip. It begins with a short ride up Coffee Creek Road. At a point beyond Benson Gulch, they turn off onto a trail that follows North Fork Coffee Creek upstream. Part way up, they reach Hodges Cabin, now a museum in the wilderness. Originally constructed in the 1920s, the eight-bedroom cabin is still in excellent shape today.

After touring the cabin, riders continue over to Saloon Creek, the site of the first saloon in the region. The spot has a historical connection with Coffee Creek Ranch, because, at one time, juice from apples grown on the ranch was fermented and turned into a potent brew. At least some of the liquor found its way to the drinking establishment at Saloon Creek.

The biggest riding event of the week is the gymkhana held on Thursday afternoons. For the competition, participants are divided by age. There are child, teenager, and adult groups. Within each group, participants compete in barrel races, balancing-an-egg-on-a-spoon races, and boot races. In the boot race, participants ride a horse to their boots, put them on, and race across the finish line. At the Thursday night awards show, ribbons are awarded to the winners.

Pack Trips

Guests may also arrange to go on an overnight trip into the nearby wilderness. A minimum of eight people is required to organize an overnight trip and guests must provide their own sleeping bags. The most popular destination for overnight trips is Lion Lake. Three meals–lunch, dinner, and breakfast–are included in the package.

Spot trips are also available for those guests who are interested. Available destinations include Conway, Lion, Foster, Union, Sugar Pine, Stoddard, and Doe Lakes.

Other Activities

When guests aren't out exploring the mountain trails of the Trinity Alps, there's plenty to keep them busy back at the ranch. They can swim in the heated pool, soak in the spa, or workout in the glass-enclosed exercise room.

They can also try their hand at badminton, volleyball, horseshoes, ping pong, shuffleboard, canoeing, or basketball. Sharpshooters can test their marksmanship at the rifle range and archers can try their skills with a bow and arrow on the archery range.

Fishing is also a popular activity at Coffee Creek Ranch. Beginners can drop a line into the ranch trout pond. More experienced anglers will prefer trying their luck in one of the nearby streams or lakes.

Hikers will appreciate the many trails around the ranch. One of the most popular hikes is the one to Stoddard Lake. Another follows the trail alongside Boulder Creek.

Each evening, the ranch staff organizes a different activity. Sunday night, they present a slide orientation about the ranch and the surrounding area. The following evening, guests play bingo.

On Tuesday night, everyone gets to kick up their heels with some old-fashioned square dancing. On Wednesday evening, guests get to ham it up in the ranch talent show and then dance to a live band. And on Thursday night, the staff presents awards to the top gymnkana performers and to other surprise recipients. Other evening activities during the week include bonfires and hay rides.

During the winter months, the ranch offers guided cross-country ski touring, ice skating, sledding, and ice fishing. Skis and skates must be provided by guests. No rentals are available at the ranch. Sleds, however, are provided.

Accommodations

The red, wooden cabins at Coffee Creek Ranch are rustic, but comfortable. Tucked away in the trees behind the main lodge, the cabins all have either a fireplace or pot-bellied stove. The interior walls of the cabins are paneled with pine and most have ceiling fans.

The cabins come in three configurations–one bedroom, one bath; two bedrooms, one bath; and two bedrooms, two baths. The later two are intended for families, with some units able to hold as many as eight people. Taken all together, the ranch can accommodate 50 guests a week.

In the summer, the one-bedroom, one-bath cabins are $595 a week for adults, $575 a week for teenagers 13 through 17, and $475 a week for children twelve and under. During the spring and fall, the rates for the same cabins are $500 for adults, $480 for teenagers, and $380 for children. The daily winter rates are $119 for adults, $115 for teenagers, and $95 for children.

The weekly summer rates for the two-bedroom, one-bath cabins are $605 for adults, $585 for teenagers, and $485 for children. The weekly spring and fall rates are $510 for adults, $490 for teenagers, and $390 for children. The daily winter rates are $121 for adults, $117 for teenagers, and $97 for children.

The summer weekly rates for two-bedroom, two-bath cabins are $615 for adults, $595 for teenagers, and $495 for children. The spring and fall weekly rates are $520 for adults, $500 for teenagers, and $400 for children. The daily winter rates are $123 for adults, $119 for teenagers, and $99 for children.

Dining

The cooks at Coffee Creek Ranch pride themselves on the quality of the meals they prepare, all from scratch. The fruits and vegetables are always fresh and the bread is homebaked.

Dinner is normally served buffet style in the main dining room. Typical entrees include roast beef, turkey with all the trimmings, stuffed filet of sole, shrimp kebabs and beef ribs, and chicken.

Lunches, sometimes served by the pool, feature menu items like hamburgers, hot dogs, Mexican cuisine, and soup with sandwiches.

Breakfast is served in the main dining room and can include items like pancakes, eggs, bacon, sausage, French toast, oatmeal, dry cereal, and omelets.

Horse Rental Rates

The two-hour rides, the breakfast rides, the picnic ride, and the gymkhana are $25 each. The all-day ride is $50. Riding lessons are $15 for a half hour. Guests may also pay a flat $200, which covers all riding for a week, with two exceptions. The gymkhana and riding lessons are not included in the weekly rate.

All-inclusive overnight trips are $100 per person. Spot trips are $135 per day for the packer and $55 a day for each saddle or pack animal.

Payment Method

Coffee Creek Ranch accepts personal checks, traveler's checks, Discover, and American Express.

Rider Age Limit

Riders must be at least five years old for all rides. No one under eight, however, is permitted to go on the all-day trip. Lessons are available for children as young as four.

Nearest Airport

The nearest commercial airport is located in Redding. However, private pilots may fly into Trinity Center Airport.

How To Get There

From Redding, take Highway 299 to Weaverville. Turn on to Highway 3 and follow it north to Trinity Center. Look for Coffee Creek Road on the left, eight miles north of Trinity Center. Turn left on Coffee Creek Road and go four and a half miles up the road. Look for the ranch on the right hand side.

WILDERNESS PACKERS
P.O. Box 405
Happy Camp, CA 96039
(916) 493-2793
Owners: Tom & Stacey Head

YOUNG'S RANCH RESORT
Somes Bar, CA 95568
(800) 552-6284
(916) 469-3322
Owners: Bob & Judy Young

Journalist I. A. Reynolds may have best captured the unique quality of the Marble Mountain region of northwest California in an article he wrote back in 1875. It was, he said, a place of "craggy heights, towering upward from amid deep, dark forests of evergreen,...lonely and unfrequented lakes,...wild and foaming streams,...and rocky cliffs, forming lofty cascades."

Over 100 years later, little about the area has changed. The same serene beauty and rugged charm that caught Herbert Hoover's attention in the 1920s, still beguiles visitors even today. Now federally protected, thanks to the efforts of Hoover, the 214,500-acre Marble Mountain Wilderness has become a favorite destination for those seeking a wilderness experience without the typical crowds.

What makes it even more appealing for trail riders, is that you can enjoy your wilderness experience on the back of a horse. Wilderness Packers working in cooperation with Young's Ranch Resort offer scenic pack trips into the Marble Mountain Wilderness and entertaining day rides along the Klamath River from May through October each year.

Wilderness Packers provides the horses and wranglers for the trips, while Young's Ranch Resort handles the reservations for day rides and provides special accommodation packages for pack trip participants.

The half-day and all-day trail rides both start at or near Young's Ranch Resort, originally the site of an old gold mining camp. On the half-day trip, riders take a loop trail up behind the ranch, where they discover pleasant backwoods scenery that few but Native Americans and the occasional gold miner have ever seen.

The Klamath River near Somes Bar

Along some stretches of the trail, riders catch views of the mighty Klamath River as it twists and turns through the canyon below. Once the exclusive province of the Karuk Indians, who lived in villages along its shores, it later attracted prospectors who sought gold in its many gravel bars. Remarkably, there are still Karuks living in the Klamath area even today, some continuing to practice their ancient rituals at the sacred ceremonial grounds at Somes Bar.

After roughly three hours in the saddle, the group completes its loop back down to Young's Ranch Resort.

On the all-day trip, riders travel along the river itself. Starting at the Halverson Creek Trail Head, located a short distance downstream from the ranch, riders take the River Corridor Trail, following the Klamath River upstream. From the trail, they have an upclose view of the river, at times flowing calmly through tranquil pools and at other times roaring through the rocks in a torrent of white water.

Looking up as they go, riders may spot an osprey as it goes into a dive or a majestic blue heron soaring overhead. Glancing back toward the water, they may also notice river otters frolicking near the shore. Continuing upstream, riders pass old cabins, reminders of the area's bygone days.

Eventually, they swing up from the river and proceed to Frog Pond Lake, where everyone gets a chance to relax and enjoy a picnic lunch prepared by the outfitters. After finishing their meal, the group travels back to Young's Ranch Resort in motorized transportation.

For vacationers interested in accommodations along with their all-day trail ride, Young's Ranch Resort offers a package that includes a private cabin and all meals for two nights. The package is designed for groups of four or more people. A second package provides food and lodging for three nights along with the trail ride and an all day river rafting trip.

Pack Trips

The most exciting trips, however, are the overnight adventures into the Marble Mountain Wilderness. The standard three- and five-day all-inclusive trips, intended for no more than eight people, can be arranged directly through Wilderness Packers. Special packages that include accommodations are available through Young's Ranch Resort.

For the most complete Marble Mountain Wilderness experience, vacationers should consider the five-day trip. Starting from the Elk Creek Trailhead near Sulphur Springs Camp Ground, riders travel through varied, sometimes rocky, often forested terrain. Along the way, riders cross several mountain streams and pass deep pools and gentle cascades. Throughout the first day, they continue to climb, at times rather precipitously.

Eventually, they reach Blue Granite Lake, sitting beneath Peak 6864 at 5,370 feet in elevation. The picturesque lake nestled amid the lodgepole pine, serves as the stopping point for the first night. At dinner, riders get a chance to sample Stacey's delicious Dutch-oven cooking. During a typical pack trip, she serves entrees like prime rib, lasagna, and pork roast. Desert can include one of her irresistible homemade cakes.

The following afternoon, the group rides for about two hours over to Ukonom Lake. As they travel, they pass through wildflower-festooned meadows and dramatic glacier-sculpted alpine terrain. At one point, they catch a brief glimpse of Mount Shasta off to the east.

For the next two nights, the group camps alongside Ukonom Lake, the largest body of water in the Marble Mountain Wilderness. During their stay, riders can try their luck with fishing; the rainbow, brook, and brown trout are plentiful. Riders can also swim, hike, ride, or just kick-back with a good book and relax. The setting is delightful, with trees all around the lake and a meadow nearby.

On the fourth day, they ride to One Mile Lake, where they camp for the last night. The following afternoon, riders complete the final leg of their journey out along the trail to Haypress Meadow.

Vacationers can also get a taste of the wilderness on the three-day trips. Starting from either Elk Creek or Haypress Meadow, riders travel to one of the three lakes visited on the longer trips–Blue Granite, Ukonom, or One Mile Lake. A base camp is established and all activities are conducted in the area nearby. On the third day, the group returns along the same trail.

For vacationers interested in additional accommodations, Young's Ranch Resort offers a special package that includes a three-day pack trip and two nights lodging, along with meals, at the resort. As a bonus, the ranch provides float tubes for fishing during the guests' stay in the wilderness.

Rates

The half-day ride is $55 per person for two people, $40 per person for three people, and $30 per person for four people. The all-day ride is $100 per person for two people, $80 per person for three people, and $65 per person for four people. There is a 20% discount for children under 11.

The special package that includes two nights in a cabin, including all meals, and an all-day trail ride is $139 per person for groups of four or more. The special package that includes three nights in a cabin, including all meals, an all-day trail ride, and an all-day raft trip is $229 per person for groups of four or more.

The three-day all-inclusive pack trip is $120 per person a day. The five-day all inclusive pack trip is $110 per person a day.

The special package that includes two nights in a cabin, including all meals, and a three-day pack trip is $459 per person for groups of two to four people.

Payment Method

Wilderness Packers accepts cash, personal checks, and traveler's checks. Young's Ranch Resort accepts cash, Visa, MasterCard, and American Express.

Rider Age Limit

There is no age limit.

How To Get There

For trips starting anywhere but Young's Ranch Resort, directions will be provided at the time you make reservations. To reach Young's Ranch Resort from the Bay Area, take Highway 101 north. At Arcata, take Highway 299 to Willow Creek. Turn on to Highway 96 and proceed to Somes Bar. Young's Ranch Resort is just north of Somes Bar on the right hand side of the road.

LAZY L RANCH

2969 Fickle Hill Road
Arcata, CA 95521
(707) 822-6736
Owners: Mark and Carrie Harnden

There are few things on the face of the earth that inspire a greater sense of awe and inspiration than the coastal redwoods of California. Entering a grove of these mighty trees, some rising over 367 feet in the air, is like walking into a house of worship. All is peaceful and quiet, with only thin bands of ethereal light streaming down.

Fortunately, despite over a century of logging, there are still places along the coast where it's possible to experience the special, hidden world of the redwoods. There's even a place where it's possible to enjoy it by horseback.

Lazy L Ranch, located in the seacoast town of Arcata, offers trail rides through a dense redwood forest in the hills above Humbolt Bay. Open Tuesdays through Sundays all year round, the Lazy L Ranch schedules one-hour, two-hour, lunch, and overnight rides.

Before leaving on the one-hour trip, riders receive basic riding instructions in the ring. Once everyone understands the rudiments of stopping, starting, and turning, the group heads into the 800-acre timber preserve adjacent to the ranch property. Though reasonably close to a residential area, the preserve is still home to deer, bears, bobcats, grey foxes, and mountain lions.

As they travel through the forest, riders get an up close view of the coastal redwoods (*Sequoia sempervirens*), the tallest living things in the world. Close cousins of the giant redwoods (*Sequoiadendron giganteum*) found in the southern Sierra, the coastal redwoods have managed to survive since the days of the dinosaurs. With a distinctive red bark that's resistant to fire, insects, and fungus, the redwood dominates all life that surrounds it.

During the one-hour trip, the route can vary depending upon the judgment of the guide. But the basic destination is always the same–a landing that overlooks Humbolt Bay. From the landing, which drops off rather precipitously, riders have a panoramic view of the city of Arcata.

First known as Uniontown, Arcata was founded in 1850 and began as a supply center for miners answering the call of the Gold Rush. Bret Harte, a resident in the late 1850s, even used the area as the setting for some of his stories. Eventually, however, logging emerged as an important industry in the region and continues as such to the present day.

Looking out towards Humbolt Bay and following the shoreline south, riders will also spot Eureka, the largest city in the northern quarter of the state. After surveying the coastal landscape, they head back through the redwoods to the stables.

Lazy L Ranch co-owner Carrie Harnden

The two-hour ride is quite similar to the one-hour trip, except riders go all the way over to the Baywood Golf & Country Club and back. On the lunch trip, available by reservation only, riders spend an hour riding through the redwoods before sitting down for a picnic lunch.

The most interesting trip, however, may be the overnight ride. Designed particularly with kids in mind, it begins with a ride through the redwoods to a special camp site. After setting up camp and eating a hearty meal, the group begins preparing for their evening under the stars. But then comes the big surprise.

Suddenly, without warning, a band of mean desperados rides into camp and shoots up the place. Ultimately, however, law and order is restored and everyone gets a good night's sleep. The following morning, the group rides back to the ranch for breakfast, having survived an attack by the toughest outlaws any cowboy has ever seen.

Rates

The one-hour ride is $15. The two-hour ride is $30. The lunch ride is $25. The overnight trip is $75 and includes two meals.

Payment Method

The Lazy L Ranch accepts cash, personal checks, and traveler's checks.

Rider Age Limit

All riders must be at least ten years old.

How To Get There

Going north on Highway 101 at Arcata, take the Samoa Boulevard exit. Turn right on Samoa Boulevard. Go to Union Street and turn left. Turn right on Fickle Hill Road. Continue to 2969 Fickle Hill Road. Look for the stables on the right hand side.

RICOCHET RIDGE RANCH

24201 N. Highway 1
Fort Bragg, CA 95437
(707) 964-7669
Owner: Lari Shea

The Mendocino coast seems like something right out of a seafaring novel. Menacing waves explode against its rocky shore. A crisp wind pins back shrubs clinging to its sandy bluffs. And creeping silently around the outstretched branches of stately pines and angular cypress is the ghostly fog. It's rugged, haunting, and quite beautiful.

The beach at MacKerricher State Park

A visit to the Mendocino coast promises long strolls on the beach, cozy meals in old wooden inns, and quiet evenings curled up by the fire. But, even more important for trail riders, it's a great place for an invigorating ride on a horse.

Ricochet Ridge Ranch, located three miles north of Fort Bragg on Highway 1, offers one-and-a-half-, three-, and four-hour rides along a nearby beach and all-day rides through a redwood forest. The ranch also arranges unique week-long, "Horse Trek Adventures," that combine rides along the beach and through the redwoods with overnight stays in quaint bed and breakfast inns.

On the one-and-a-half-hour trip, scheduled at 10:00 a.m., 12:00 noon, 2:00 p.m., and 4:00 p.m., riders cross Highway 1 and enter MacKerricher State Park. Named after a pioneering family that homesteaded the land back in 1864, the 1,000-acre park contains forests, meadows, and a long stretch of beach.

Traveling along a pine and cypress-shaded trail, riders head towards the beach. Continuing out across a bluff, they work their way down to the tideline. They don't actually go into the water, but skirt the tide as it slaps against the sand. Looking off towards nearby rocks, they spot sea lions taking a snooze. During the early part of the year, it's even possible to observe California gray whales spouting or breaching just off the coast.

They continue along the beach for some distance, with seagulls, cormorants, and the occasional great blue heron soaring overhead, before swinging up to the bluffs. After going along the bluffs on an old logging road, riders return to the beach for more sport in the sand. Upon reaching a large dunes area, they turn around for the trip back.

The standard one-and-a-half-hour ride is conducted at a walk throughout. However, riders may select to go on a private trip, where loping along the beach is permitted. Longer private rides are also available

The three-and four-hour private rides are simply extensions of the one-and-a-half hour trips. Riders have an opportunity to see more of the beach that runs through MacKerricher State Park and beyond. On the four-hour trip, for instance, riders go all the way to the mouth of Ten-Mile River, several miles up the coast.

For a different riding experience, vacationers might consider the all-day trip. It takes place in Jackson State Forest, located between Fort Bragg and Willits on Highway 20. Created for the purpose of developing and demonstrating forest management practices, the 50,200-acre forest is filled with coastal redwoods. Riders spend the day, traveling along the many old logging roads that crisscross the park, enjoying the serenity of the dense forest and the beauty of these remarkable trees. Everyone participating is provided with a picnic lunch.

Overnight Trips

The most interesting discoveries at Ricochet Ridge Ranch, however, are the Horse Trek Adventures. Combining some of the appeal of a guest ranch, with the freedom to travel to different locales, they provide a unique horseback vacation experience. Available in four-day and seven-day packages, the Horse Trek Adventures are scheduled several times each summer. Riders may use either English or Western saddles, while riding on an Arabian, Russian Orlov, thoroughbred, or quarter horse.

For the complete experience, vacationers should select the full seven-day package. It begins on Sunday, with check-in at the Cleone Lodge, located just down the road from Ricochet Ridge Ranch. Everyone then meets at the ranch for an introduction to their horses. Once everyone has been matched with the right horse, they head down to the beach for a one-and-a-half-hour ride. A Mexican dinner follows at the Purple Rose Cafe.

Monday is spent at Jackson State Forest, where riders are split into groups for walking, trotting, and loping through the redwoods. A grilled salmon or snapper dinner awaits them back at the Cleone Lodge.

Riders return to Jackson State Forest on Tuesday for additional rides along different trails. In the evening, everyone checks into the historic Mendocino Hotel, located on a bluff overlooking the ocean in the charming community of Mendocino. Built in 1878, the hotel is furnished with Victorian antiques and decorated with artifacts from the past. Visitors can then go next door to the Bay View Cafe for dinner.

Horses and riders get the day off on Wednesday. It gives everyone a chance to browse the many shops and art galleries in Mendocino. Or they can enjoy a soak in a hot tub, a refreshing massage, or a stroll along the beach. Lunch is served at the Hill House Inn, one of the locations used for the popular television show *Murder She Wrote.* Dinner in the elegant dining room of the Mendocino Hotel is followed by a private concert by classical pianist Susan Archuletta.

On Thursday, the group rides up to Ten Mile Beach and then turns inland at the river, following it upstream through a stand of redwoods. Continuing across a cattle ranch, the group stops for lunch in an apple orchard. Riders finish up the day at DeHaven Valley Farm, which provides lodging, complete with hot tub, for the balance of the week.

The group makes a loop trip back down along Ten Mile River the following day. On the return, after lunch, riders try a mini-endurance ride. They race up the ridge to DeHaven Valley Farm at a full gallop. After the ride, Lari Shea, owner of Ricochet Ridge Ranch and an experienced endurance rider, teaches the group about horse anatomy and demonstrates how to take a horse's pulse. In the evening, the group gets together after dinner for a talent show.

On Saturday, the group rides back to Ricochet Ridge Ranch along the beach. It's one last opportunity to lope through the sand and even splash in the surf. At the ranch, horses head for their stalls and riders motor back to DeHaven Valley Farm. After dinner, a local Mendocino band performs folk, cajun, and country music for the riding group's final night together.

Not everyone, of course, has seven days to spare. To accommodate those with tighter schedules, Ricochet Ridge Ranch also presents an abbreviated version of the week-long program that runs from Monday through Thursday.

The four-day program begins, as the longer one does, with a ride on the beach and a night at the Cleone Lodge. But, then, instead of riding in Jackson State Forest and spending time in Mendocino, the group heads straight up the beach to DeHaven Valley Farm. The final two days are similar to the final two days on the week-long program.

Rates

The one-and-a-half-hour ride is $23 and the private one-and-a-half-hour ride is $28. The three-hour private ride is $48 and the four-hour private ride is $58. All-day private rides are $98, including lunch.

The seven-day Horse Trek Adventure is $1560. The four-day Horse Trek Adventure is $925.

Payment Method

Ricochet Ridge Ranch accepts cash, personal checks, and traveler's checks.

Rider Age Limit

All riders must be at least six years old. Everyone under 21 years old must wear a helmet. Helmets are also available for older riders.

How To Get There

From Highway 101 at Cloverdale, take Highway 128 towards the coast. Turn onto Highway 1. Go three miles past Fort Bragg. Turn right on Mill Creek Road. Ricochet Ridge Ranch is on the corner of Mill Creek Road and Highway 1.

Early morning riders at Sunset Corral

BAY AREA 2

SONOMA CATTLE COMPANY

P.O. Box 877
Glen Ellen, CA 95442
(707) 996-8566
Owners: Gary and Arlene Nelson

From the moment he first laid eyes on the magnificent, sprawling ranch, rising up from the Valley of the Moon, Jack London knew he had found his home. From its shaded canyons and grassy hillsides to its forests of redwood, oak, and fir it was the place of his dreams. With royalties from the novel *The Sea Wolf,* the world-renowned writer, radical thinker, and rugged individualist purchased his beloved "Beauty Ranch" in 1905 and lived there until his death in 1916.

Today, a large section of the ranch, containing some of the original buildings, has been incorporated into a state park dedicated to his memory. Jack London State Historic Park, located in the town of Glen Ellen, offers visitors a unique opportunity to learn more about the man and the fascinating life he led.

It also provides visitors a way to explore the ranch the way Jack London always loved to – on the back of a horse. Sonoma Cattle Company, headquartered right in the park, offers horseback rides along the same trails that Jack London once followed. It's a special chance for anyone who loves riding to share in the spirit of the man who once proclaimed, "I am the sailor on horseback! Watch my dust!"

Operating from April through November each year, the stable offers one- and two-hour trail rides as well as lunch and barbecue trips. On the one-hour trip, riders start out from stables located at the far end of the upper parking lot. Almost immediately, they pass the ruins of an old winery and a distillery building used by the previous owners for making sherry.

During the great earthquake of 1906 it was heavily damaged, but later London adapted it for use as guest quarters and as living quarters for the ranch hands. A fire in 1965 gutted the upper floors and only ruins remain today.

The nearby distillery building, completed four years after the winery, was used by London for storing farm equipment. The "Cottage," located behind the winery, served as London's personal living quarters. It was there that he wrote many of his stories and novels, and where he died of an accidental overdose of morphine, taken for medical reasons, on November 22, 1916.

Riders then swing over past "Pig Palace," an unusual piggery designed by London to save labor. The ranch was, of course, quite experimental in nature and London was constantly looking for new and innovative ways to raise livestock and crops.

Continuing along the trail, riders pass two 40-foot high grain silos that were once used to store feed for the livestock.

As they go around the corner of a private vineyard, owned by London's heirs, riders will pick up the Lake Trail. Looping around the five-acre lake, originally constructed as a farm irrigation reservoir, riders pass the redwood log bathhouse where London and his wife once entertained friends. They then return back down the Lake Trail to the stables.

The two-hour ride starts along the same route, but at the lake it continues on to Mays Clearing. Sitting as it does on the side of Sonoma Mountain, it offers riders a spectacular view that includes the north end of San Francisco Bay and Mount Diablo beyond.

They continue on down Fallen Bridge Trail to the park boundary and then onto state hospital land. Picking up State Hospital Orchard Trail, they ride through an orchard of pears, apples, plums, and apricots. Then they return to the park.

Along the way, riders will catch sweeping views of the city of Glen Ellen and out across the valley to the mountains on the other side. Eventually, they reach a magnificent redwood forest that contains at least one tree that's over 1,500 years old. They then complete the final leg of the journey back to the stables.

On the lunch trip, intended for groups of six or more, riders travel either to a spot in the state hospital orchard, to the bathhouse, or to one of the upper meadows. At the luncheon spot, everyone sits down for a special box lunch meal provided by the stables. Typically, the lunch trip lasts about three hours.

Groups of ten or more people might consider the barbecue ride. For this special trip, riders travel to a campground nestled in the redwoods. With a western band providing the musical entertainment, the group enjoys an old-fashioned barbecue featuring either chicken or steak, along with cowboy beans, tossed salad, and dessert.

Additional Facilities

Sonoma Cattle Company also offers trail rides throughout the year at nearby Sugarloaf Ridge State Park, 2,700 acres of rolling hills, chaparral, and grasslands.

The shortest of these, the one-hour ride, is probably only appropriate for small children or for those with limited experience in the saddle. On this trip, riders follow a simple loop route that meanders through the grasslands and live oaks in the valley, once the home of the Wappo

Indians. It's quite peaceful, but riders miss the views they'd enjoy on the two-hour trip.

On the two-hour trip, they climb to the ridge of a nearby hill. Looking out from the ridge, riders have a panoramic view of Sonoma and Napa Counties. They will catch a view of Mount Diablo and on a clear day they can even spot the Sierra Nevada. They then loop back down through the center of the valley, where deer can often be seen grazing.

Sonoma Cattle Company also offers special sunset and moonlight rides. On the sunset ride, participants have an excellent ridgetop view as the sun drops down behind the ocean. Riders also travel to the top of a ridge on the moonlight trip, returning along a trail illuminated only by a lunar glow.

Sugarloaf Ridge State Park

Rates

The one-hour ride is $20. The two-hour ride is $30. Sunset and moonlight rides are $35. Lunch rides are $50 and barbecue rides are $60. There is also a five-dollar per car admission fee to enter either of the state parks. A sign posted at the stables encourages tipping.

Payment Method

Sonoma Cattle Company accepts cash, personal checks, and traveler's checks.

Rider Age Limit

All riders must be at least eight years old.

How To Get There

From Highway 101 at Petaluma, take Highway 116. Turn off on to Highway 121 and proceed north. To enter Jack London State Historic Park, take a left on London Ranch Road in Glen Ellen. Follow the road up into the park. Look for the stables at the far end of the upper parking lot.

To reach Sugarloaf Ridge State Park, continue on past Glen Ellen and turn onto Highway 12. Go north on Highway 12 and look for the state park entrance on the right. Follow the road from the park entrance all the way to the end. Look for the stables on the right.

ARMSTRONG WOODS PACK STATION

P.O. Box 970
Guerneville, CA 95466
(707) 887-2939
Owners: Jonathan and Laura Ayers

There's something rather dark and mysterious about the redwood forest at Armstrong Woods State Reserve. In among the tall trees, densely clumped together, it's shadowy, silent – a place where mischievous goblins or an evil sorcerer might appear. But besides providing stimulation for one's imagination, it's really quite peaceful and serene.

Originally established as "a natural park and botanic garden" back in the 1870s by wealthy lumberman, Colonel James Armstrong, the 700-acre reserve features coastal redwoods, the tallest living things in the world.

Immediately adjacent to the reserve is Austin Creek State Recreation Area, more open and airy, featuring grassy hills dotted with oak, bay, and madrone. Taken together, these two diverse areas offer greatly varied countryside for sightseeing on a horse.

Fortunately for vacationers, Armstrong Woods Pack Station is available to provide the rides. Open year round, the pack station arranges half-day, all-day, and three-day trips by advance reservation through Armstrong Woods State Reserve and Austin Creek State Recreation Area. Rarely are there more than six to eight people on a ride.

All rides begin at the pack station, located within the state reserve. On the half-day trip, riders head out along the Pool Ridge Trail, snaking their way through the towering redwoods to the end of the canyon. Moving into the 4,200-acre Austin Creek State Recreation Area, they slowly climb out of the redwoods and into grassland.

The air becomes warmer and the surroundings drier. Away from the redwoods, tangled brush known as chaparral begins to appear. Further into the wilderness, wild turkeys are sometimes seen along the trail. Deer and even the occasional mountain lion also appear.

Eventually, riders reach Horse Heaven, a large meadow on the site of an extinct volcano, where they take in a view of Mount Tamaplais to the south and Mount Diablo to the southeast. After watering the horses from a mountain spring and resting, they return down the same steep trail.

There are two choices for the all-day trip. Riders can either go up past Horse Heaven to the top of 1,940-foot-high McCray Mountain or they can swing off the Pool Ridge Trail to Gilliam Creek.

Riders looking for a magnificent view might prefer the McCray Mountain trip. On a clear day, they can see the Pacific Ocean in one direction and the Sierra Nevada range in the other. In addition, they have a sweeping panorama of several nearby counties to enjoy. The Gilliam Creek ride offers pleasant wilderness scenery and the chance to relax in a hammock under a shade tree with the stream flowing by. Both rides feature a picnic lunch prepared by Laura Ayers. Frequently, she serves barbecued chicken and salad.

Pack Trips

For those looking for a longer stay in the wilderness, Armstrong Woods Pack Station also offers three-day trips up to Mannings Flat on East Austin Creek. On the first day of the trip, riders eat a continental breakfast at the pack station before hitting the trail. Then they saddle up and begin the climb out of the redwood reserve.

From McCray Ridge, they drop down to Mannings Flat Camp, a pleasant, shaded spot overlooking East Austin Creek. Just beyond is a beautiful meadow, always covered with colorful wildflowers in the spring. While in camp, riders can curl up in a hammock to relax or play with the river otters in a nearby swimming hole.

At dinner, riders sit down to a delicious meal served by candlelight. At mealtimes, the emphasis is always on healthy foods made with fresh ingredients, but prepared with a gourmet flair.

The following morning, they go for a morning ride up to the top of 1,378 foot high Fox Mountain. After enjoying lunch with an accompanying view of the surrounding area, they ride back down to camp in time for an afternoon swim.

On the third day, they follow East Austin Creek down to the spot where it forks with Gilliam Creek and then return to the pack station along the Gilliam Creek Trail.

Rates

The half-day ride is $35. The all-day ride is $70. Three-day all-inclusive pack trips are $350 per person.

Payment Method

Armstrong Woods Pack Station accepts cash, personal checks, and traveler's checks.

Rider Age Limit

There is no set limit; however, riders under 10 years old must have previous riding experience.

How To Get There

From Highway 101 north of Santa Rosa, take the River Road exit to Guerneville. Proceed on Highway 116 to Guerneville. In Guerneville, turn right on Armstrong Woods Road. Proceed to Armstrong Redwoods State Reserve. Inside the reserve, follow "Horses for Hire" signs to the pack station.

SEA HORSE STABLES

P.O. Box 277
2660 Highway 1
Bodega Bay, CA 94923
(707) 875-2721
Owner: Marcy J. Heiman

Over the long span of his illustrious career, Alfred Hitchcock managed to forever link a number of famous American landscapes with scenes of horror and suspense.

Probably no Hitchcock film has a stronger association with a particular locale, than the one that exists between the 1962 thriller, *The Birds,* and the community of Bodega Bay. Movie memories, however, are just one of the reasons to visit Bodega Bay. Even more appealing are its many charming old buildings, its wind-swept vistas, and its scenic rocky coast.

Best of all for trail riders, you can enjoy Bodega Bay's unique charms from the back of a horse. Sea Horse Stables, open every day but Thanksgiving, Christmas, and New Years, offers guided trail rides in the rolling hills above Bodega Bay and along its picturesque shore.

On the one-hour trip, riders head out across a portion of the ranch's 700 acres of wide, open pasture land. From a distance, they can look back and appreciate the simple elegance of the white-frame ranch buildings sitting out in the open with the rolling, green hills behind them. Framed in one's mind, the whole scene has the smooth, clean feel of an Edward Hopper painting.

Traveling at a pace never more vigorous than a trot, riders will reach Salmon Creek at the northeast corner of the ranch property. From there, they climb into the hills behind the ranch buildings. Looking out from this slightly-elevated vantage point, riders can see the coastline stretched out below them and Bodega Bay's harbor just to the south. They complete their loop by dropping back down to the stables.

Sea Horse Stables

During the summer and fall, when the water in Salmon Creek is low, Sea Horse Stables offers a two-hour ride up the creek. As with the one-hour trip, riders travel through the pasture to Salmon Creek. But then, instead of heading into the hills, they follow the creek canyon upstream. The narrow trail is, at times, somewhat treacherous, so Sea Horse Stables discourages inexperienced riders from going on this trip.

After following the trail upstream for some distance, riders climb to the top of the hills from the back. They continue along the surprisingly flat ridgeline, taking in the spectacular view of the coastline as they go. Then they work their way back down to the stables.

There is a second option for the two-hour trip and it's the one many people prefer – the beach ride. It begins with riders going down the driveway to the edge of Highway 1. When it's safe in both directions, they cross the road and continue on into the Salmon Creek Beach area. After riding through the grassy dunes, they reach the beach and proceed to travel along the tideline for about 20 minutes. Some horses are even comfortable going into the water.

During the early months of the year – February through April– riders can watch the gray whales go by. The most common sight is of spouting, but riders can sometimes spot a whale breaching the water. Seals also make an appearance from time to time. Other animals often seen in the dunes area are deer and jackrabbits. Seagulls and red-tailed hawks are frequently observed riding air currents overhead.

After enjoying the beach, riders return to the stables along a different trail. Those preferring more time in the saddle may add a ride through the hills at the end of the trip.

One thing to consider before riding at Bodega Bay is the weather. It can be quite cold and windy, particularly along the beach. For the best riding conditions, plan on visiting the area in the fall. It's warmer, less windy, and there is much less fog.

When planning a trip to the area, vacationers might also consider the Bed & Breakfast facilities at the ranch. The comfortable, moderately-priced rooms offer either ocean or mountain views. Write to the ranch for more details.

Rates

The one-hour ride is $20 and the two-hour rides are $35. Longer rides are $10 for each additional hour. Guests of the Bed & Breakfast receive a ten percent discount.

Payment Method

Sea Horse Stables accepts cash, personal checks with I.D., traveler's checks, Visa, and MasterCard.

Rider Age Limit

All riders must be at least eight years old.

How To Get There

From Highway 101 at Petaluma, take the East Washington Street exit. Make a left on East Washington and stay on it all the way out to the coast. Eventually, it merges with Highway 1. Go two miles north of the town of Bodega Bay and look for Sea Horse Stables on the right.

FIVE BROOKS STABLES

1000 Highway 1
Olema, CA 94950
(415) 663-1570
Owner: Fred Vaughn

There's something rather unusual about Pine Gulch Creek and Olema Creek located in the Five Brooks area of Point Reyes National Seashore. Though they run essentially parallel, they do so in opposite directions. The cause for this seemingly inexplicable occurrence, however, is easy to explain. The hidden hand that has radically altered the geology of the region is none other than the San Andreas Fault, running along the eastern border of the Point Reyes park.

Upon closer examination, the impact of the fault becomes apparent in other ways as well. For instance, Point Reyes is built on granite, while the rock foundation of the land east of the fault is of the sedimentary Franciscan Formation. Also a study of other streams in the area reveals that some make odd right-angle turns as they flow through the earthquake zone. As it happens, a spot near Point Reyes was the epicenter of the 1906 San Francisco Quake.

But earthquake faults and unusual geology are not the only reasons to visit the Point Reyes National Seashore. It's also a place of great scenic beauty, abundant wildlife, and interesting places to explore. There is also an excellent way to explore them. Five Brooks Stables, open throughout the year, offers guided trail rides of various lengths through portions of Point Reyes National Seashore.

The shortest of these, the one-hour ride, is offered at 10:00 a.m., 11:00 a.m., 1:00 p.m., 2:00 p.m., and 4:00 p.m. Departing along the Stewart Trail, an old logging road, riders go around Five Brooks Lake, home to ducks, pied-billed grebes, hooded mergansers, and green-backed heron.

Farther along, the trail leads past Stewart Camp Ground and across the infamous San Andreas Fault. During the 1906 earthquake, lateral movement along this benign appearing fault moved some houses and other structures in the area as much as 15 feet.

Continuing, the path goes behind the Stewart Horse Ranch, where Morgan horses and Angus cattle are raised. Now operated by the third generation of the Stewart family, the ranch has buildings on it that date back to 1863. From the ranch, riders complete the loop back to the stables.

On the two-hour ride, scheduled at 9:00 a.m., 12:00 noon, and 3:00 p.m., riders make the gradual climb through the thick forest to Inverness Ridge. At 1,324 feet in elevation, they reach Firtop, a wide meadow surrounded by Douglas fir. The density of the forest is one of the unique characteristics of the Point Reyes area. Another is that redwoods are entirely absent. Its unusual geological composition is offered as the explanation for both phenomenon.

From Firtop, riders will head south along the Ridge Trail. Looking off through occasional openings in the forest, they can catch views of the Pacific Ocean. At the junction with the Bolema Trail, they begin the rather steep descent back down into the valley. Along the way, they can see Mount Tamaplais off in the distance. The Olema Valley Trail, running parallel with Highway 1 and coincidentally with the San Andreas Fault, takes them back to the stables.

Riders head out along a different trail for the three-hour ride, offered at 9:00 a.m. and 1:00 p.m. Steeper and narrower than the Stewart Trail, the Greenpicker Trail is a slightly shorter route up to the top of the ridge. At Firtop, riders swing onto the Glen Trail and continue to Glen Camp, traveling through a meadow, across a stream, and past a small pond. At one point, there is a view of the ocean through the trees. At Glen Camp, riders rest under the shade of Douglas fir, before returning to Firtop and making the more gradual descent back to Five Brooks along the Stewart Trail.

The most interesting trip, however, is the all-day ride, starting at either 9:00 or 10:00 a.m., that goes out to Wildcat Beach. Beginning along the Stewart Trail, riders work their way up to Firtop. They then make the rather steep descent down to Wildcat Camp. Surrounded by coastal scrub, but no trees, the camp sits just above the beach.

Providing that the weather and the tide cooperate, riders continue out to Wildcat Beach. They spend 20 to 30 minutes exploring the small expanse of sand as it's pounded by the surf. The horses from Five Brooks Stables, however, will not go in the water. Given the rather cool temperatures along the shoreline, few riders would want to go in the water either.

Back at Wildcat Camp, everyone dismounts for a half-hour picnic lunch, food being provided by individual riders. On the return trip, the group takes an unmarked trail to a junction with the Bolema Trail. They drop down the Bolema Trail and then complete their trip along the Olema Valley Trail.

Rates

The one-hour ride is $15. The two-hour ride is $25. The three-hour ride is $40. The all-day ride is $55.

Payment Method

Five Brooks Stables accepts cash, traveler's checks, Visa, and MasterCard.

Rider Age Limit

There is no specific age limit, but all riders must be tall enough to reach the stirrups.

How To Get There

From Highway 101, take the San Anselmo exit. Head west on Sir Francis Drake Blvd. to the town of Olema. Turn left onto Highway 1. Go south approximately five miles. Look for the stables on the right hand side of the road.

MIWOK LIVERY

701 Tennessee Valley Road
Mill Valley, CA 94941
(415) 383-8048
Owner: Linda Rubio

Home first to cannons, then 16-inch guns, and finally Nike-Hercules missles, the rolling, green hills of the Marin Headlands have provided defense for San Francisco Bay since back in the 1870s. But as times changed along with the nature of warfare, the facilities became obsolete. In 1972, approximately 42,600 acres of former military property in the Marin Headlands were incorporated into the Golden Gate National Recreation Area, and today they are available for all to enjoy.

Some parts of it are accessible by automobile, of course. There are also wonderful trails for scenic strolls to the beach. But for getting up on the ridge line to experience the views, there's no better way than by horseback.

Miwok Livery, located in the Tennessee Valley, offers one-hour trail rides by advance reservation every day but Monday. Limited to no more than four people, the rides are available on either English or Western saddles. Riders using English tack, however, must wear regulation helmets and traditional riding boots.

As the trip begins, riders head off along a dirt road, lined with pine trees, that winds up the side of a hill. Looking off to the left as they make their slow climb, riders have a magnificent view of 2,604-foot high

Mount Tamaplais. Nestled down below is the charming community of Mill Valley. Originally the site of Marin County's first saw mill, the town today provides its upscale citizenry with just the right mix of country living and cosmopolitan culture.

Eventually, the road reaches Wolf Ridge. Though two hills in the foreground prevent a completely unobstructed view of San Francisco, riders can see out across the western end of the city.

Looking off from the Marin Headlands towards San Francisco

As riders continue up the road, the trees thin out and only occasional tufts of brush poke out of the grassy hills. Off in the distance, riders can spot the San Rafael Bridge. Stretched out below them is a finger of land known as the Tiberon Peninsula with Angel Island State Park just beyond. The East Bay is clearly visible from points further up

the road and the houseboats of Sausalito come into view immediately below.
the western end of the city, particularly down along the Great Highway. One of the towers of the Golden Gate Bridge can also be seen poking up through a notch in the hills. While perched up on the ridge, it's not uncommon to see a red-tailed hawk drift by. Other wildlife seen in the recreation area include bobcat, deer, and grey fox.

After a brief stop, riders return back down the hill following a slightly different trail. As they work their way down through the grass and brush, they catch sight of the Pacific Ocean off to the left beyond the rolling hills. Immediately in front of them is an even better view of Mount Tamaplais. At the bottom of the hill, they swing around to the stables.

One thing to consider before a ride in the Marin Headlands is the weather. Wolf Ridge is in the heart of the fog belt and on many days of the year there is no view at all. It's much less of a problem during the cool winter months, however. Regardless of the season, it's a good idea to dress in layers, because the temperatures can change dramatically as you climb from the valley to the ridge.

Rates

The one-hour ride is $25.

Payment Method

Miwok Livery accepts cash, personal checks, and traveler's checks.

Rider Age Limit

Riders must be at least 12 years old.

How To Get There

From Highway 101 just north of the Golden Gate Bridge, take the Stinson Beach exit. Turn left on Tennessee Valley Road. Follow it to the Golden Gate National Recreation Area parking lot. Turn left at the lot and proceed to the stables.

SUNSET CORRAL

2901 Vineyard
Novato, CA 94947
(415) 897-8212
Owners: Pat and Gail Martin

For thousands of years, the Miwok Indians lived a peaceful, productive life in villages all around Marin. Left undisturbed, their simple life of hunting and gathering might have continued right to the present day. Unfortunately, the arrival of Spanish missionaries in the late 1700s marked the beginning of the end of Miwok culture. By the time of the Gold Rush, there was virtually nothing left of it.

Today, most of what remains from that era is to be found in museums. But there's one thing that the Miwoks gave to Marin that even time and the onslaught of modern civilization couldn't erase—their ancient system of trails. Along the trails they once blazed, it's still possible to follow in the footsteps of the Miwok Indians.

Of course, one of the best ways to follow the old trails is by horseback. Sunset Corral, located in the sunny, inland community of Novato, offers trail rides through nearby hills first explored by the Miwoks. The guided rides, ranging in length from a half hour to a half day, are normally limited to a walk or trot. Groups made up exclusively of experienced riders may, however, do some loping when the terrain permits.

The half-hour trip is primarily intended for individuals with limited riding experience. It offers them the opportunity to get their boots in some stirrups for the first time, without pushing them to do more than feels comfortable. They also get to enjoy a pleasant ride into a dense grove of redwoods, where only wisps of sunlight filter through. Upon reaching a hitching post that's been installed in the grove, the group turns around and comes back.

The one-hour ride is just an extended version of the half-hour trip. After traveling through the redwoods, riders climb through the grass-covered hills to a ridge that provides views of the surrounding area. Looking around, riders can spot the city of Novato, the Indian Valley Golf Course, and, on a clear day, San Francisco Bay.

By adding an additional half-hour to the hour trip, riders can continue along a trail above the golf course. From the trail, they get a closer look at the 212-acre course and catch views of Stafford Lake.

Riders enjoy even better views on the two-hour ride. However, the trip is not recommended for beginners. It's a tough, steep climb to a landmark called Ship's Mast. Along the way, riders pass through a section of redwoods and beds of fern. Other portions of the trail pass through fields of grass that turn green and fill with wildflowers in the spring.

The principal reward for the climb, though, is the view at the top. Besides excellent panoramas of Novato, Ship's Mast also provides views of the bay, weather permitting. The vistas are particularly impressive as the sun goes down, so the stable schedules a special ride to Ship's Mast at sunset.

Those looking for more time in the saddle might consider the half-day trip. From the stables, riders take the trail that goes past Indian Valley Golf Course and up the grassy slopes of Mount Burdell. The route offers riders an opportunity to travel over varied terrain, making it an interesting ride. There are also stretches on this trip where experienced riders can lope.

Once on top of the small mountain, riders have a sweeping view of the whole Bay Area. Among the landmarks, they can spot Mount Tamaplais to the south and Mount Diablo out across San Pablo Bay. Looking north, they can see into Sonoma County.

On their return to the stables, they can get in a few more lazy lopes.

Rates

The half-hour ride is $10 and the one-hour ride is $17. The one-and-a-half-hour ride is $25 and the two-hour ride is $32. Two-hour sunset rides are $37. Half-day rides are $60. A sign at the stables encourages tipping the guide.

Payment Method

Sunset Corral accepts cash, personal checks from Marin banks, and traveler's checks.

Rider Age Limit

Riders must be at least five years old and be comfortable on a horse. The stables will make judgments on a case by case basis.

How To Get There

From Highway 101, take the Atherton Avenue exit. Continue west on San Marin Drive. Eventually, it becomes Sutro. Turn right on Vineyard Road and go to the end.

WILD HORSE VALLEY RANCH

P.O. Box 229
Napa, CA 94559
(707) 224-0727
Owner: California Resort Clubs, Inc.

There was time back before the turn of the century, when mustangs roamed wild and free through the hills just east of Napa. Like their counterparts still found in the deserts of the Southwest, their lineage could be traced to the horses first brought to the New World by early Spanish explorers. Unfortunately, the wild horses of southeastern Napa County were not to survive.

Considered troublesome and destructive by the cattle ranchers who came to the region in the 1890s, the spirited horses were rounded up and destroyed. Now, all that remains of their legacy, is the name given to the area where they once lived–Wild Horse Valley.

Maybe it's poetic justice then, or just somewhat ironic, that today this peaceful, secluded valley up in the hills above Napa has become one of the leading equestrian centers in Northern California. Western training center for the United States Equestrian Team and a full-service boarding and riding stables, Wild Horse Valley Ranch has made the area the primary domain of horses once again.

Best of all for vacationers, Wild Horse Valley Ranch offers trail rides at 9:00 a.m., 11:30 a.m. and 2:00 p.m., every day but Tuesday, throughout the year with advance reservations. The guided rides, two-hours in length, are conducted at the pace of the slowest rider, so loping is permitted, if everyone in the a group is capable. Typically, groups number no more than six people.

With over 3,000 acres of ranchland at their disposal, riders have an opportunity to experience varied terrain. Following a loop route around the ranch, they ride through grassy meadows, into shady groves, and up rugged hills. The landscape is classically Californian with rolling hills, either green, golden, or brown, depending on the season, surrounded by stands of gnarled oak. It's a place where deer can frequently be observed and where birds are constantly seen.

During the two-hour trip, riders also pass vineyards that cover many acres of land just beyond the ranch's borders. The presence of grape growing should not come as a surprise, of course, given Napa County's reputation as one of the leading wine producing regions in the world. But it may prompt some riders to consider one of Wild Horse Valley Ranch's catered rides.

Designed for groups of 15 or more people, the brunch, lunch, or dinner trips all begin with a ride out to Leoma Lake. There riders are met by a crew from Food For Thought, a Napa catering company, and they sit down to a delicious meal.

The brunch menu typically features scrambled eggs with salsa, hash browns, sausage, and mimosas–orange juice mixed with champagne. Menus for the other meals can include entrees like grilled flank steak with peanut sauce, grilled chicken pieces with fruit salsa, or grilled pork tenderloin with apple chutney. Salads, mixed vegetables, homemade breads, and desserts are part of every meal. Of course, fine Napa wine is always served. It all makes for a relaxing way to enjoy beautiful Napa County.

Rates

The two-hour ride is $25. Brunch, lunch, and dinner trips are from $50 to $65 per person, depending upon the menu selected.

Payment Method

Wild Horse Valley Ranch accepts cash, personal checks, traveler's checks, Visa, and MasterCard.

Rider Age Limit

All riders must be at least eight years old. All riders under 18 must wear a helmet.

How To Get There

From Highway 80 East, transition to Highway 37. Take the Napa exit. Follow signs into Napa. Turn right on Highway 121. Turn right on Coombsville Road, which becomes Wild Horse Valley Road. Follow signs to the ranch.

D & F PACK STATION

1525 Castle Rock Road
Walnut Creek, CA 94598
(510) 946-1475
Owner: Brad Myers

At first glance, there's little about Mount Diablo in Contra Costa County that seems particularly remarkable. Its gently-rounded countenance is visible from many spots in the Bay Area, of course. It also dominates the landscape that immediately surrounds it. But, at a mere 3,849 feet in elevation, it seems a fairly insignificant geological lump in a state that boasts the Sierra Nevada.

What it lacks in size, however, it more than makes up for in location. Because, sitting as it does just east of San Francisco, with no other mountains of comparable size nearby, Mount Diablo provides the best 360° view found anywhere in North America. Only Mount Kilamanjaro in East Africa offers a more spectacular view in all the world.

Fortunately, for vacationers, the view from Mount Diablo is also quite accessible. You can even drive there. But anyone who enjoys adventure, natural scenery, and the great outdoors is going to be much happier climbing Mount Diablo on the back of a horse.

D & F Pack Station, located nearby, offers trail rides of various lengths through Mount Diablo State Park, including an all-day trip to the top of the mountain. Open all year, the pack station is operated by Brad Meyers, owner of D & F Pack Station at Huntington Lake in the central Sierra.

The shortest ride available, the two-hour trip, is offered at 9:00 a.m.,

11:30 a.m., and 2:00 p.m. Leaving from the pack station, riders travel first through Diablo Foothills Regional Park for about a mile, before entering Mount Diablo State Park. Following a loop trail, they travel through a narrow canyon, shaded with oaks, that is home to deer, quail, and grey fox. Continuing up into the rolling foothills, riders have views off in the distance of Martinez and Concord as well as nearby Walnut Creek.

Riders gain more elevation on the four-hour ride, scheduled at 8:00 a.m. and 1:00 p.m. each day. Heading out on an old stage coach road through Pine Canyon, they pass Pine Pond, where ducks can be seen paddling around. Emerging from the pine- and oak-shaded canyon, they continue through a landscape typical of California with rolling, grass-covered hills and occasional oak trees.

Eventually, they reach Barbecue Terrace, near the state park headquarters. From this spot, sitting at 1,800 feet in elevation, riders can see across to San Francisco Bay. After a rest, they return down the same trail.

A special barbecue ride up to Barbecue Terrace is also available for groups of 10 to 25 people. While riders enjoy the view, wranglers cook up juicy tri-tip steaks for the hungry throng.

The ride not to be missed, however, is the all-day trip, because that goes right to the top of Mount Diablo. Following the same route as the four-hour trip, riders climb through the hills to Barbecue Terrace. From there, they take the Summit Trail on up to the top.

On a clear day, you may not be able to see forever, but it will almost feel like it. Over 40,000 square miles are visible from the top of Mount Diablo. Of the 58 counties in California, riders can see parts of at least 35 counties. Off to the northeast, they can spot Mount Lassen, some 185 miles away, and with binoculars, they can even pick out Mount Shasta. Looking east across the San Joaquin Valley, they catch a panoramic view of that geologic wonder, the Sierra Nevada. Using binoculars, riders can even peek into Yosemite Valley and make out the unmistakable, glacier-sculpted shape of Half Dome.

Mount Hamilton and Mount Loma Prieta are visible to the south. Then swinging around, riders have a breathtaking view of the Golden Gate Bridge, Mount Tamaplais sitting just north of it, and the Farallon Islands out to sea beyond.

Needless to say, the best time to visit Mount Diablo is just after a rain storm, when the air is crystal clear. It's probably best to avoid the area during the summer. Typical summer days are quite hot and air quality generally deteriorates under those conditions. There is also little tree cover there, making the riding conditions on a hot summer day unpleasant for horse and rider alike.

Rates

The two-hour ride is $20 and the four-hour ride is $35. The all-day ride to the top of Mount Diablo is $60. The barbecue ride is $50. There is a sign near the pack station office that encourages riders to tip the guide.

Payment Method

D & F Pack Station accepts cash, personal checks, traveler's checks, Visa, and MasterCard.

Rider Age Limit

Riders must be at least six years old. Younger riders may double with a parent.

How To Get There

From the East Bay take Highway 24 east. Transition onto Highway 680 north. Take the Ygnacio Valley Road exit. Go east on Ygnacio Valley Road for three miles. Turn right on Oak Grove Road. Eventually it turns into Castle Rock Road. Look for 1525 Castle Rock Road on the left.

GOLDEN GATE PARK STABLES

P.O. Box 22401
San Francisco, CA 94122
(415) 668-7360
Owner: Polly Dignan

Back in 1870, when work began on Golden Gate Park in San Francisco, there was little to suggest that the project would ever amount to much more than a civic embarrassment. The 1,017-acre area of land set aside for the park was sandy, windswept, and bereft of vegetation.

What emerged on the spot, once called "a dreary waste of shifting sand hills," is, therefore, truly remarkable. Golden Gate Park, today, is one of the most beautiful urban parks to be found anywhere in the world. With its lush meadows, elegant promenades, and colorful gardens, Golden Gate Park is a visual delight for all who visit it.

Exploring the park, of course, can be done in a number of ways, but none are more enjoyable than on the back of a horse. Golden Gate Park Stables, open Tuesday through Sunday from 9:00 a.m. to 5:00 p.m., offers one-hour trail rides through a northwest section of the park. The rides, available with either English or Western saddles, must be reserved in advance.

With many different bridal paths crisscrossing the park, the route may vary, depending upon the judgment of the guide. However, typically, the ride includes the buffalo paddock and Spreckels Lake in its itinerary. Departing from the stables, located behind the polo field, riders normally head west along the bridal path that skirts the police department stables and follows John F. Kennedy Drive. They continue past the Angler's Lodge and the fly-casting pool, constructed in the 1930s by the WPA.

Golden Gate Park Stables gives "get along little doggies" a new meaning

Crossing John F. Kennedy Drive, riders reach the buffalo paddock and follow a trail that goes around behind it. Looking through the chainlink fence, they observe the big, shaggy-coated animals grazing, resting, or just standing around. Continuing along the trail, shaded by eucalyptus, they emerge into the open area around Spreckels Lake, where they may be greeted by a few disapproving geese. Popular with model boat enthusiasts, the man-made lake is usually dotted with radio-controlled craft; their skippers directing the mini-voyages from the nearby shore.

Riders circle the lake and recross John F. Kennedy Drive. As they do so, they have an opportunity to observe one of the many beds of rhododendrons found in the park. After enjoying this one last burst of color, riders complete their all-to-brief journey back to the stables.

Rates

The one-hour ride is $18.

Payment Method

Golden Gate Park Stables accepts cash and traveler's checks only.

Rider Age Limit

Riders must be at least eight years old.

How To Get There

From Highway 101, take the Park Presidio exit near the Golden Gate Bridge. Proceed south on Park Presidio to Golden Gate Park. Turn right on John F. Kennedy Drive. Look for the stables near 36th Avenue.

FRIENDLY ACRES STABLES
P.O. Box 279
Half Moon Bay, CA 94019
(415) 726-9916
Owner: Al Shipley

SEA HORSE RANCH
P.O. Box 279
Half Moon Bay, CA 94019
(415) 726-9903
Owner: Al Shipley

Smugglers loved Half Moon Bay back during the days of Prohibition. Isolated from major cities and neatly protected by its curving shores, the bay provided ideal surroundings for offloading bootleg whiskey and rum. Times, of course, have long since changed. Now the only spirits associated with the area are those found in the famous Half Moon Bay pumpkin patches during Halloween.

But, even if the wild times of the rumrunners are long gone, there's still one way to find excitement down on the beach. Half Moon Bay is one of only a handful of places in California where vacationers can go horseback riding through sand, seaweed, and surf.

Friendly Acres Ranch and Sea Horse Ranch, operating under the same ownership, offer guided and unguided trail rides through the nearby state park and down along the beach. Both stables are open seven days a week from 8:00 a.m. to 6:00 p.m., closing an hour earlier in the winter. Selecting between the two, located less than a quarter mile from each other, is virtually a coin-toss, although Sea Horse Ranch is closer to the beach.

On all rides, a guide serves as an escort part of the way, but then riders are on their own. For an additional charge, a guide will remain with riders for an entire trip. Even when unsupervised, however, riders are expected to go no faster than a walk or a trot.

The easiest and safest ride for beginners is the one-hour trip. It stays up on the bluffs above the beach. Departing from either of the stables, riders travel south through Half Moon Bay State Park. Following a level trail through open fields and past stands of cypress, they have sweeping views of the bay off to their right. Upon reaching the park's entrance area at the southern end of the park, they turn around and come back to the stables along the same trail.

Riders interested in getting down on the beach should consider either the one and-a-half-hour or the two-hour ride. They are essentially the same trip, except one allows riders more time on the beach.

Both begin along the same trail used for the one-hour ride. However, upon reaching the park entrance, riders continue south along the bluffs for some distance. Eventually, they reach a spot where the trail drops down to Poplar Beach, a wide stretch of sand virtually devoid of rocks. Once on the beach, riders may take their horses along the tidelines. If their horses are willing, they can even plunge into the rolling surf.

While riding along the beach, riders can also enjoy the splendid view. From Poplar Beach, they're able to see up and down the coast. Most prominent of the nearby landmarks is Pillar Point, jutting out like a stubby finger at the north end of the bay. After spending time on the beach, riders make their return trip along the same trail they took out.

A special barbecue ride is also available for groups of ten or more riders. After working up an appetite on a one-and-a-half-hour, guided beach ride, the group returns to the stables for a catered barbecue. Steak is the main course for a meal that includes baked beans, baked potatoes, and soft drinks.

Rates

The one-hour ride is $20. The one-and-a-half-hour ride is $28 and the two-hour ride is $35. The barbecue ride is $50. Dinner for non-riders is $15. Guides are $18.

Payment Method

Friendly Acres Ranch and Sea Horse Ranch both accept cash, in-state checks, and traveler's checks.

Rider Age Limit

Riders must be at least six years old.

How To Get There

Traveling north on Highway 1, look for Sea Horse Ranch off to the left, one mile north of Half Moon Bay. Friendly Acres Ranch is only a short distance farther up the road on the left. Traveling south on Highway 1, look for the two stables on the right.

GARROD FARMS

22600 Mount Eden Road
Saratoga, CA 95070
(408) 867-9527
Owner: Jan F. Garrod

Long before the Santa Clara Valley became known for silicon chips, floppy disks, and computer companies started in garages, this warm, fertile region was one of the world's leading fruit producers. Prunes, cherries, and apricots flourished in orchards all across the valley, as the Gold Rush, and the flood of immigrants that followed it, provided a growing demand.

It's not too surprising, then, that when David Garrod purchased 65 acres in the hills above Saratoga back in 1893, he quickly grew an orchard. Over the 70 years that followed, Garrod Farms was an active and successful fruit producer. Today, though it no longer maintains the orchards, it continues to grow grapes on its current 120 acres.

But it's not fruit trees or grapevines that attract people to Garrod Farms. It's the chance to enjoy one of the few undeveloped corners in the Santa Clara Valley on horseback.

With full stables and an active equestrian program, Garrod Farms offers one of the best riding programs in the area. Residents and vacationers may choose either English or Western saddles for unguided rides around the ranch and across the adjacent Fremont-Older Preserve. Boots are required for those choosing to ride English.

Open seven days a week throughout the year, Garrod Farms requires advance reservations on the weekends. Actual riding time is limited only by the endurance of the riders and the amount they are willing to spend. All charges are based on an hourly rate. During their time on the trail, riders may walk or trot, but running is not permitted.

From the stables area, riders take off along one of several trails over a steep hill. They can choose to go up alongside the vineyards or over past a small pond. From the top of the hill, the trail continues on to the nearby 575-acre preserve, a part of the Mid-Peninsula Regional Park District

Traveling through oak trees and dry chaparral along a ridgeline in the foothills of the West Valley, riders have views that on a clear day can extend over seven counties. Looking up past San Francisco, they can spot Mount Tamaplais. Off to the northeast, Mount Diablo can be seen. Of course, they also have a sweeping view of the whole Santa Clara Valley and the tangle of development on both sides of San Francisco Bay.

Within the preserve, there's an opportunity to follow a loop trail through varied terrain at the pace of each rider's choosing. When an individual rider or group has had enough, they can simply point their horses in the direction of the stables and ride back.

Rates

The basic charge is $20 per hour. For groups of ten or more people, the rate is $15 per hour.

Payment Method

Garrod Farms accepts cash, traveler's checks, and Visa.

Rider Age Limit

All riders must be at least nine years old.

The Garrod Farms vineyards

How To Get There

From Highway 17, take the Los Gatos exit. Take Highway 9 towards Saratoga. Continue on Highway 85, also known as Saratoga-Sunnyvale Road. At Pierce Road, turn left. Proceed to Mount Eden Road and turn right. Follow Mount Eden Road to Garrod Farms.

Tracking down a stray at Spanish Springs Ranch

NORTHEASTERN COUNTIES 3

SPANISH SPRINGS RANCH

P.O. Box 70
Ravendale, CA 96123
1-800-272-8282 (In Calif.)
1-800-228-0279 (Outside Calif.)
Owner: R.C. "Bob" Roberts

Somehow the sky just seems bigger in northern Lassen County. Maybe it's the sparseness of the population or the vast, wide-open plains. But it feels like a place where you could ride until sundown and never meet a soul.

Not surprisingly, it's a great place to raise cattle, which they've been doing there since the 1860s. Over the years, ranches have come and gone, but very little about the area has really changed.

There is one thing, however, that has changed–it's now possible for city folks to join in on the fun. Spanish Springs Ranch, a 70,000-acre spread near Ravendale, offers probably a greater range of guest facilities and all-year-round ranching experiences than can be found anywhere else in California.

It is, in reality, not just one ranch, but a collection of ranches, that owner Bob Roberts, a builder from Marin County, has acquired over the last 25 years. The headquarters ranch, bearing the Spanish Springs name, is really a western resort, offering modern amenities with a cowboy theme. At the same time, some of the other ranches operated by the Robert's company are virtual museums of cowboy history, thoughtfully preserved and carefully maintained.

What's great for guests is that they can select the level of comfort versus authenticity that they want. They can stay in a modern suite near a pool and a tennis court or in a 75-year old farmhouse with kerosene lamps for light.

Certainly, every effort has been made to insure that a stay at the main Spanish Springs Ranch is both comfortable and memorable. There's a full list of activities, with the most important activity, of course, being horseback riding. Several riding events are planned daily.

The routes on the 5,297 foot high ranch change each time out, but generally, riders travel for an hour or two through the nearby sagebrush-covered hills and valleys. One day, riders head down to Lopez

Meadows for a lunch cookout and another day to the top of Spanish Springs Peak, which provides a panoramic view of the Madeline Plains.

Back at the ranch, they can take riding lessons at the rodeo arena. In addition, if any work needs to be done with the 5,000 head of cattle on the ranch, guests are invited to join in.

Other Activities

After guests are finished riding for the day, they can hop on the hay wagon and help feed the horses. Or, if they prefer, they can play a set of tennis or grab some rays by the pool. Down at the pond, which has been stocked with bass and trout, they can fish on a catch and release basis. Other activities at the ranch include trap shooting, archery, pool, shuffleboard, horseshoes, and roping lessons.

Guests can also drive out towards the Cold Springs Ranch and observe the ranch's herd of buffalo grazing in the nearby pasture.

In the late afternoon, they can join other guests for a beer and wine happy hour in the lounge next to the dining room. On Saturday nights, they can two-step to the beat of a live country and western band, and on Sunday nights they can do a little square dancing.

One of the big events of the week, particularly for kids, is the Dudeo. Staged in the rodeo area, children and adults participate in events including PeeWee Stick Horse Races and everybody's favorite, Mutton Busting, a sheep riding competition. Awards for the top participants are given out in the evening.

In the wintertime, guests can ride in a horse drawn sleigh, ice skate, sled, or cross country ski.

Accommodations

Spanish Springs Ranch can accommodate as many as 65 people at one time. Guests stay in modern, comfortable duplexes, log cabins, suites, or bunk houses.

The duplexes have one queen bed, one twin and a private bath. The log cabins come with a bedroom and a loft. The suites feature a bedroom and a small living room equipped with a refrigerator and a wet bar.

Larger families may prefer the bunk houses. Mom and dad stay in a private room and the kids sleep in the 14-bed girls and boys dorms.

Duplexes and bunk houses are $100 per day for adults and $50 per day for kids four through 12. Log cabins and suites are $125 per day for adults and $50 per day for kids. Children under four stay free.

All meals and most activities are included in the basic rate. An extra 15 percent is added to the bill to cover all gratuities.

Dining

Meals are served in the attractive, modern dining facility that also serves as a public restaurant for people passing through the Ravendale area. While enjoying a view out over the Madeline Plains, guests feast on tasty entrees like steak, chicken, seafood, lamb chops, and prime rib along with vegetables, soup, and salad.

In addition, the ranch also stages lunch and dinner cookouts and a big barbecue on the patio next to the dining room.

On Sunday mornings, the ranch presents a champagne buffet brunch that has become so popular that people drive all the way up from Susanville to join in.

Other Ranches

For those interested in an even more authentic cowboy experience, Spanish Springs Ranch also manages several other ranches in the area. All are interesting, but the real gem is the Marr Ranch. Started back in 1891 by George and Thomas Marr, this remote 5,000-acre ranch, tucked away in Box Canyon, was once a major supplier of horses to the U.S. Calvary.

Today, the two-story ranch house, built out of stone some 75 years ago is charmingly furnished with old antiques and cowboy memorabilia. Of course, it also lacks electricity.

Sleeping accommodations are available upstairs and also in the more recently constructed bunkhouses nearby. In all, the ranch can hold 20 people at any one time, with eight staying in the main house. The rates are $100 per day for adults and $50 per day for kids.

During the day, guests work with the cattle and horses. In addition to the normal gathering activities, they also help with branding at least once during the week. When there are no specific ranch chores, guests are able to go out on trail rides.

In the evening, everyone gathers around the old dining table for a home-cooked meal that's as delicious as it is filling. The quality of the cooking is a source of pride with the host and hostess and they warn that the Marr Ranch is no place to come if you want to stay on a strict diet. After dinner, guests sit in the rocking chairs on the porch and watch the sun set off in the west. Then they return inside to do a little two-stepping in the kitchen

During the winter months, guests come to the Marr Ranch to cross country ski and to enjoy an unforgettable Thanksgiving dinner or old Victorian Christmas.

Guests who would prefer to be completely on their own might consider either the Horne Ranch or the Evans Ranch. The Horne Ranch, which dates back to the 1870s, has a house that sleeps four people and rents for $500 per week. The Evans Ranch, from the same era, has a three-bedroom house that sleeps eight people and rents for $700 per week. Two horses, linens, pots, and pans are provided at each place. Guests bring their own food.

Those who want to step even farther back in history, can sleep in a tepee. The tepees, located on the Cold Springs Ranch property, will sleep up to five people and rent for $65 per day. The use of a horse, however, is an additional charge. Spanish Springs Ranch also owns additional property with guest facilities across the border in Nevada.

Cattle Roundups

The truly adventurous, who want an even bigger taste of the cowboy life, might consider joining the crew for the spring and fall cattle roundups. Would-be wranglers are awoken at the crack of dawn and spend long hours in the saddle tracking down the cattle and separating them by brand. Small calves are sorted out from cows with older calves, ready to be weaned and mother cows are separated out according to when they'll give birth.

It's tough, demanding work out in the sagebrush and juniper, but it's a way to find out if you've got what it takes to be a cowpoke. Participants stay at either the Roberts Ranch, the Marr Ranch, or Soldier Meadows in Nevada. Occasionally, they even sleep under the open sky. Normally, a participant signs up for a week.

Cattle Drives

Once the cattle are rounded up, it's time for the spring or fall drive. For folks from the big cities and suburbs, this is a *City Slickers* fantasy come true. Seven tough days are spent on the trail, as the cattle are driven 80 miles from the winter grazing area in Nevada's Black Rock Desert to the Madeline Plains. In the fall, it takes seven more days to drive them back.

Around 20 guests are invited to come along and help on each drive. They sleep in communal tents, rise at first light, and work the cattle long into the day. Lunch is served from a chuck wagon and dinners are cooked over an open fire.

Horse Drives

Considered by many to be the most exciting riding event around, horse drives have quickly grown in popularity. Spanish Springs Ranch conducts two five-day drives each spring to distribute 80 head of horses to the Marr, Evans, Horne, and Cold Springs Ranches.

Between 15 and 20 guests are invited to help out. As with the cattle drive, guests sleep in tents and eat meals around a campfire. The main difference, of course, is that the horses can really fly. Participants without prior riding experience may find this a bit harrowing.

Pack Trips

During the summer months, Spanish Springs Ranch also offers all-inclusive pack trips into the Warner Wilderness. Leaving from Cold

Springs Ranch, riders travel through scenic wilderness country with meadows full of wildflowers, groves of aspen, and gurgling springs. It's an opportunity to enjoy a camping experience away from the kinds of crowds that are found in other parts of the state.

Horse Rental Rates

The basic room rate includes the use of a saddle horse during a stay at Spanish Springs Ranch or the Marr Ranch. The cattle roundups are $100 per day and the seven-day cattle drives are $950. The five-day horse drives are $550. All-inclusive pack trips are $350 for three days and $550 for five days.

Payment Method

Spanish Springs Ranch accepts cash, personal checks, traveler's checks, Visa, MasterCard, and American Express.

Rider Age Limit

All riders must be at least seven years old. A baby-sitter is available, at an additional charge, to look after smaller children.

Nearest Airport

The closest commercial airport is located in Susanville. Private pilots, however, may fly into Ravendale.

How To Get There

From Reno, head north on Highway 395. Continue 45 miles past Susanville. Just outside of Ravendale, look for the prominent Spanish Springs Ranch sign on the right. Follow the private road up to the ranch.

DRAKESBAD GUEST RANCH

Lassen Volcanic National Park
Chester, CA 96020
(Winter Address)
2150 N. Main #7
Red Bluff, CA 96080
(916) 529-1512
Owners: John and Pam Koeberer

The Drakesbad Ranch had already been in existence for many years when on Memorial Day in 1914, a nearby volcano, Mount Lassen, awoke from a long slumber. Its eruption was so powerful and the curiosity it generated so enormous, that in 1916, Lassen Volcanic National Park was created.

The birth of the new park caused a change at the Drakesbad, as well. Many of the new visitors to the area would seek out rental horses at the Drakesbad for trail rides up Mount Lassen. With this new influx of tourists, the ranch was transformed into the rustic resort of today.

Now part of the national park and open from early June through early October each year, the Drakesbad Guest Ranch offers vacationers a restful environment where they can relax and unwind. Located near a scenic meadow and a natural hot spring, at 5,680 feet in elevation, the ranch appeals primarily to people who prefer fewer activities and more unstructured time.

It also appeals to people who enjoy riding a horse. Each day during their stay, guests have an opportunity to go on trail rides of different lengths to various locations within the park.

The shortest of these, the one-hour ride, is a simple loop through the meadow near the ranch. Carpeted with wildflowers through early July, the meadow is home to a number of marmots and attracts many deer. Riders travel up over a nearby slope, cross Hot Springs Creek, and continue briefly along the Boiling Spring Lake Nature Trail. Eventually, the trail brings them back through the meadow near the Drakesbad swimming pool, which is fed by a natural hot spring.

The main lodge at Drakesbad Guest Ranch

On the one-and-a-half-hour trip, riders travel down through the meadow and on over to Devil's Kitchen, where everyone gets off their horses for a half-hour self-guided tour. Walking through the geothermal site, riders get a close-up look at the mudholes, hot springs, and steaming fumaroles that dot the area. They then return along the meadow trail that leads past the swimming pool.

The two-and-a-half-hour trip follows portions of the one-hour trail, but then riders continue on down through rocky, volcanic terrain to view Terminal Geyser, actually a steam-spouting fumarole. After observing the thermal activity, including some mudholes, they return along the same route followed by the other trips.

On the four-hour trip, riders travel down to Terminal Geyser and then continue on to Willow Lake, which sits surrounded by pine trees and a large meadow.

The premiere ride, however, is the three-and-a-half-hour trip that goes to Sifford Lakes and to Kings Creek Falls. Besides getting a chance to photograph the picturesque 50-foot high falls and one of the scenic lakes, riders also catch an excellent view of Mount Lassen along the way.

Other Activities

When they're not out riding, guests can hike, fish, swim in the hot spring-fed pool, or sit on the porch of the old lodge and read a book. They can also play ping pong, volleyball, or horseshoes.

On Friday night, a park ranger leads a nature walk, and every evening there's a campfire, where guests roast marshmallows and sing songs.

Accommodations

The Drakesbad can accommodate up to 75 guests. They stay in brown, wood-sided buildings that resemble park service housing. All have gas stoves, sinks, toilets, and kerosene lamps. Some have private baths. The beds in the rooms are all hand made.

Cabins and lodge rooms with a half bath are $102 per person per day for one person in a double bed. The rate is $76 per person per day for two persons in a double bed or a double and a single. Each additional person is $66 and children two through 11 are $54.

Bungalows with two double beds and a private bath are $116 per person per day. Two people are $85 per person per day. Each additional person is $70 and children are $54.

Duplexes, two rooms with a connecting bath, have two double beds in one room, a double bed and a single bed in the other, and are intended for groups of four. The rates are $91 per person per day for two people. Each additional person is $70 and children are $54. All meals and most activities are included in the basic rate.

Dining

Mealtimes are a pleasure at the Drakesbad Guest Ranch. They are served in the charming pine-paneled dining room that features hand-made furniture, and a pot-bellied stove. The style is gourmet, but the emphasis is on healthy. The chef uses only fresh vegetables and serves entrees like prime rib, halibut, Cornish game hen, and pasta.

Breakfasts feature French toast with fruit on top, eggs, bagels, nine-grain cereal, pancakes, and sausage. The sack lunches that are prepared each day for riders and hikers contain sandwiches, fruit, and Drakebad's popular chocolate chip cookies.

Horse Rental Rates

The first hour is $20 and each additional hour is $12.

Payment Method

The Drakesbad Guest Ranch accepts cash, personal checks, traveler's checks, Visa, and MasterCard.

Rider Age Limit

Riders must be at least nine years old officially, though there is some flexibility in individual cases.

Nearest Airport

The closest commercial airport is in Redding. Private pilots can fly into Chester.

How To Get There

From Interstate 5 at Red Bluff, take Highway 36 east. At Chester, take Warner Valley Road into Lassen Volcanic National Park. Follow the road all the way to the end.

GREENHORN CREEK GUEST RANCH

2116 Greenhorn Ranch Road
Quincy, CA 95971-9204
1-800-33-HOWDY
Owner: Murray Howard

Lake Almanor is to the north of it, Donner Lake is to the south of it, and almost nothing but miles of forest lie in between. Located in the scenic Feather River country the Greenhorn Creek Guest Ranch offers city-weary families a place to get away from it all. Open from the end of March through the end of November, the ranch, sitting at 4,000 feet in elevation, can accommodate as many as 103 people.

end of November, the ranch, sitting at 4,000 feet in elevation, can accommodate as many as 103 people.

It is not, however, a ranch in the traditional sense. Developed on a parcel of land within a subdivision of vacation homes, it more closely resembles a summer camp. In many ways, it's run like a summer camp, too, with a schedule jammed packed with activities that are very much geared to families. In particular, a real effort is made to keep pre-teens and teens, notorious for a low tolerance of boredom, occupied.

In keeping with the western theme of the place, the number one activity is, of course, horseback riding. Each day at 10:00 a.m. and 2:00 p.m., guests go out on trail rides in groups divided according to ability–beginning, intermediate, and, if necessary, advanced.

A Greenhorn Creek Guest Ranch wrangler heads out on the trail

Beginners are instructed in basic starting, stopping, and turning skills and, by the end of the week, they are permitted to trot. More experienced riders go on steeper, more rugged trails and have many opportunities to lope. There are also lots of different places to ride. The nearby Plumas National Forest provides guests with literally thousands of acres of interesting terrain. They ride through thick forests of pine and fir, up on scenic ridges, across grassy meadows, and alongside meandering creeks. Guests also go on a dinner ride to a nearby meadow and on a lunch ride to a spot overlooking a creek.

Other Activities

When they're not out on the trail, guests have plenty of other activities to keep them occupied. They can go on a gold prospecting trip to one of the nearby rivers, for instance. On these excursions, they're taught the correct technique for panning gold and usually they'll find at least a trace of gold dust. When they get tired of prospecting, they can jump in the river for a swim.

Back at the ranch, young anglers can try their hand at fishing down at the old fishing hole behind the recreation room. It's been conveniently stocked with rainbow trout and catfish, so even beginners are sure to have good luck. Older anglers will probably prefer the greater challenge provided by the nearby lakes and streams.

Guests can swim in the pool or play in an organized volleyball game. Other activities include horseshoes, ping pong, badminton, pool, board games, video games, and Capture The Flag. Golfers can get in some swings and tennis players can hit a few balls at the nearby Feather River Inn.

There's also a Kiddie Corral, under the supervision of an activities director, that provides special activities, including pony rides for children ages three to five.

On Wednesdays, the ranch stages a rodeo for the guests that includes barrel races, an egg toss, and a sack race. After the rodeo, everyone participates in a softball game. Then, in the evening, each guest catches a frog and frog races are staged in the recreation room.

Two nights a week, a caller comes in to teach square dancing and on Thursday night, a live band performs "everything from Willie Nelson to AC-DC." A game night with black jack, poker, and dice games is also organized.

Accommodations

Guests can either stay in one of 16 rustic one-and two-bedroom units–some in duplexes, others in fourplexes–or in one of the twelve one-bedroom units in the main lodge. Designed with wood-paneled interiors in a western motif, all come complete with private bathrooms.

Depending upon the number of bedrooms and the bed arrangement, they can hold anywhere from three to six people.

Weekly rates range from $455 to $620 for adults depending upon the time of year. Rates for teenagers range from $385 to $545. Rates for children through age 12 range from $355 to $515. All meals and activities are included in the basic rate.

A number of special discount programs apply to these rates. There are discounts for senior citizens, for repeat guests, for guests who make referrals, and for guests who pay in full 30 days before arrival.

Dining

The Greenhorn Creek Guest Ranch serves good, wholesome meals that should satisfy the fickle tastes of all members of the family. Typical entrees include pork chops, fried chicken, burritos, turkey, and steak. Breakfasts feature blueberry pancakes, eggs, french toast, and omelettes. Lunches generally tend to be light.

Horse Rental Rates

The basic room rate includes the use of a saddle horse during the stay at the ranch.

Payment Method

The Greenhorn Creek Guest Ranch accepts cash, personal checks, traveler's checks, money orders, MasterCard, Visa, Discover, Diners Club, and American Express.

Rider Age Limit

All riders must be at least six years old. They must be at least 13 years old to ride with the intermediate group.

Nearest Airport

The closest commercial airport is located in Reno, Nevada. Private pilots, however, may fly into Quincy.

How To Get There

From Reno, head north on Highway 395. At Hallelujah Junction, head west on Highway 70. Look for Greenhorn Ranch Road, 12 miles east of Quincy. Turn right and follow the road up into the Greenhorn Ranch subdivision. Look for the guest ranch on the right.

The view of Donner Lake from the summit

LAKE TAHOE 4

SUMMIT CORRAL

P.O. Box 9281
Truckee, CA 96162
(916) 426-3622
Owner: Bill McGuire

By now, the story of the Donner Party's long desperate winter back in 1846-47 has become the stuff of legend. Driven by starvation, several members of the group were reduced to cannibalism. Of the original 89 who began the journey, only 47 survived.

These days, Donner Pass no longer poses much of a challenge. Vacationers in their automobiles race over the top in minutes. But for those who still possess a bit of the pioneering spirit, there is a more old-fashioned way to explore the countryside around Donner Pass.

Summit Corral, located just past the summit on Highway 40, offers trail rides from June through September each year that provide spectacular views of the whole Donner area. Starting times for rides are flexible and riders have two basic trips to choose from–one and two hours in length.

On the one-hour trip, riders head out towards an overlook point above Lake Angela, before continuing to a spot just above the Donner Summit marker, siting at 7,088 feet in elevation. Standing on top of the mass of granite that forms the famous summit, riders have a magnificent picture-postcard view of Donner Lake, Truckee, and the mountains that surround them. This has to rank as one of the best photo opportunities in the Donner region.

The ride continues through the Donner Ski Ranch. Some sections of this area are relatively flat, and riders with the proper experience and ability may gallop. From the ski area, they return to the corral.

The two-hour ride follows essentially the same route as the one-hour trip, except one additional loop is added.

Summit Corral also offers a service that is unique in California. Vacationers may lease a horse for a week or for an entire summer. Essentially, this means a rider can have unlimited access to a particular horse for a flat fee.

Rates

The basic charge for rides is $15.00 per hour. For more information about the horse leasing program, write to Summit Corral.

Payment Method

Summit Corral accepts cash, personal checks, traveler's checks, Visa, and MasterCard.

Rider Age Limit

All riders must be at least eight years old.

How To Get There

From Truckee, take Highway 40 west past Donner Lake. Continue up through Donner Pass. Look for the Summit Corral just beyond the summit on the right, near Donner Ski Ranch.

SQUAW VALLEY STABLES

1525 Squaw Valley Road
Olympic Valley, CA 96146
(916) 583-7433
Owner: Squaw Valley Stables, Inc.

The prospectors came first, hunting unsuccessfully for gold back in the 1860s. They were followed soon after by the farmers. But it wasn't until developers transformed this great natural amphitheater into a ski resort in the 1950s, that Squaw Valley, site of the 1960 Winter Olympics, finally came into its own.

Squaw Valley Stables, located in the heart of the valley, offers trail rides from mid-May to mid-September that travel all over the resort. As stables go, the Squaw Valley operation is more active than most and by necessity one of the best organized. Wranglers carry walkie-talkies to communicate with each other, even when they are out on the trail. There is a strict time schedule for the rides, and groups are moved onto the trail with the kind of precision you might find at Disneyland.

Unfortunately, the trip that most people select, the one-hour ride, doesn't have a whole lot to offer. Every hour on the hour from 9:00 a.m. to 5:00 p.m., riders head out across the meadow, over Squaw Creek, and up a road towards the old ski jump. They then head east along a trail that follows the lower tree line.

As they reach a point that overlooks the golf course, riders drop down to a lower trail and head west again, riding essentially parallel with the road on which they just traveled. Eventually, they cut across the meadow, over Squaw Creek, and back to the stables.

A much better choice for a one-hour ride would be the private trip. It costs more, but it also offers more. One wrangler even considers it the best ride at Squaw Valley. Heading off to the northeast, riders go past the tram building and the Tram Condominiums. Continuing, they follow Squaw Creek up a sandy trail into Shirley Canyon.

There, inside the canyon, riders discover a beautiful waterfall tumbling into a pool. Adding to the idyllic scene are a profusion of wildflowers that create a picturesque rock garden. After enjoying the splendors of the canyon, riders work their way back down to the stables in the valley.

Three times a day–9:30 a.m., 11:30 a.m., and 2:30 p.m.–Squaw Valley Stables offers a two-hour ride. On the morning trips, riders take off along the same trail used for the one-hour ride. But instead of turning around at the old ski jump, they continue on to the end of the valley and then up a ski slope, following a small creek. Eventually, they reach Lookout Point, where they catch a view of the entire valley, before returning down Mountain Run to the stables.

In the afternoon, the wranglers take a somewhat different route. Heading south, riders cross the meadow and then continue up the side of the tree-covered hill that forms the valley's southern wall. They climb to a ridge on the southside that provides them with a view overlooking the central portion of the valley. After enjoying the view, they head back down.

The three-hour trip, offered once a day at 1:30 p.m., follows the same route as just described with one important difference. Instead of stopping, riders continue up the ridge to a spot where an old picnic table sits. From there, they have an excellent view down into Alpine Meadows, the valley immediately south of Lake Tahoe. They rest, take pictures and then return down the mountain.

The longest ride of the day is the half-day trip. It departs at 10:30 a.m. After crossing the meadow and passing the old ski jump, riders head up one of the ski runs at the end of the valley. Following this route, they climb all the way up to the High Camp Bath and Tennis Club at the top of the cable car system. During their half-hour stay at the 8,200 foot high complex, riders may eat at one of the restaurants and enjoy the breathtaking view. They then return down the steep trail to the stables 2,000 feet below.

Squaw Valley Stables also offers a breakfast ride every morning at 8:30 a.m. It follows the standard one-hour loop through the meadow. When riders return, they're served a breakfast that includes a fruit cup, cowboy scrambled eggs, ranch-style potatoes, homemade muffins, along with a choice of either sausage or bacon, and either coffee or tea.

Rates

The basic charge for rides is $15 an hour. The breakfast ride is $22 and the private one-hour ride is $25. A sign near the office announces "Tips Welcome."

Payment Method

Squaw Valley Stables accepts cash, personal checks up to $60, traveler's checks, Visa, and MasterCard.

Rider Age Limit

Riders must be at least six years old and there are no exceptions.

How To Get There

From Tahoe City, take Highway 89 north. From Truckee, take Highway 89 south. From either direction, look for the signs to Squaw Valley Ski Area. Go west on Squaw Valley Road, and look for the stables on the left.

ALPINE MEADOWS STABLES

P.O. Box 357
Tahoe City, CA 95730
(916) 583-3905
Owner: Larry Courtney

Just over the ridge from Squaw Valley, in an area surrounded by thick forests and high mountain peaks, sits Alpine Meadows, the second largest ski resort in the North Tahoe region. Its 2,000 acres of skiable terrain and over 100 different runs lure skiers from all over.

Now Alpine Meadows has something that attracts visitors during the summertime as well. Alpine Meadows Stables, located a half mile up from Highway 89 on Alpine Meadows Road, offers one-hour, two-hour, and half-day trail rides around the ski resort area. The stables, which are open only during the summer months, operate 9:00 a.m. to 6:00 p.m. daily, without an organized schedule. Reservations, however, are recommended.

The one-hour ride goes in a big loop through the dense fir and pine forest that covers the hills near the stables. Heading off to the north, riders climb a small ridge and then swing down in the direction of the Truckee River. At one point during the trip, the river comes into view. Riders then continue looping around. On their return to the stables along a trail that is lined with large granite boulders, they cross a small creek.

Riders gain more elevation on the two-hour trip. The trail heads off west through the thick forest in the direction of Scott Peak, looming 8,246 feet off in the distance. Along the way, riders have an excellent view of the valley. They can see what remains of the old ski area and the new development that has been added. The trip back to the stables is mostly downhill.

More ambitious riders might consider the half-day trip. Following a trail that goes up and over the ridge to the south, riders come down to Page Meadows. Upon reaching the meadows, riders stop for a half hour to eat lunch. Then they return back up the ridge and over to the stables.

Rates

The one-hour ride is $14 and the two-hour ride is $25. The half-day trip is $45.

Payment Method

Alpine Meadows Stables accepts cash and traveler's checks.

Rider Age Limit

Riders must be at least five years old.

How To Get There

From Tahoe City, take Highway 89 north. A short distance down the road, look for the sign for Alpine Meadows. Turn left on Alpine Meadows road and proceed for one-half mile. The road to the stables is on the left.

NORTHSTAR STABLES

Northstar Drive
Northstar, CA 95734
(916) 562-1230
Owner: Teresa K. Cartellieri

Half way between the small mountain town of Truckee and the shores of Lake Tahoe sits Northstar-at-Tahoe, one of the most beautiful and environmentally-sensitive ski resorts you'll ever find anywhere. The Sierra Club has praised it and intermediate skiers love it.

Now trail riders have the opportunity to meander through the same tree-covered hillsides and wide-open meadows that cross-country skiers enjoy so much in the wintertime. Northstar Stables, open year round, offers rides along the many trails that wind through the 2500-acre resort. Open from 9:00 a.m. to 5:00 p.m. in the summer and from 10:00 a.m. to 4:00 p.m. in the winter, Northstar Stables takes out groups of riders every hour on the hour, except 1:00 p.m.

The first ride of the day is the breakfast ride. It's a 45-minute trip through the forest and down the Porcupine Trail to a clearing below the Northstar gas station. From this view spot, riders can look out over the expanse of the Martis Valley and the Martis Creek Wildlife Area. After enjoying the view, they head back up to the stables for a breakfast that typically consists of eggs, hash browns, sausage, biscuits, coffee, and juice.

The regular 45-minute ride follows this route during the cool morning hours. When it begins to warm up, the wranglers switch to a shaded trail that winds through the forest above the stables. Climbing up a ridge then they return back down to the stables.

There is even more elevation gain during the one-and-a-half-hour ride. On what is essentially an up and back trip, riders travel through the thick forest of white fir, lodgepole pine, and sugar pine to the Northstar reservoir. Sitting just below Sawmill Flat, it offers views of the nearby Northstar Ski Area.

Northstar Stables also offers a half-day trip for experienced riders. Beginning along a trail that skirts the Northstar golf course, they cut over to Highway 267. In one quick move, riders cross the road and then head off to the south through the woods towards Klondike Meadows. Along the way, they can spot Dry Lake through the trees. After reaching the meadows, they loop back towards the stables.

The last ride of the day is the dinner ride. As with the breakfast trip, riders go out on one of the 45-minute trails and then return for dinner at the stables.

During the wintertime, Northstar Stables continues to operate, weather permitting. The thick forest offers a beautiful setting for a ride through the snow.

Additional Facilities

The owner of Northstar Stables also offers one- and two-hour trail rides at the Tahoe-Donner Equestrian Center in nearby Truckee. Unfortunately, a fire in 1959 destroyed many of the trees in the immediate area and even today it hasn't fully recovered. There are some thick stands of alder in places, but the hillside used for the rides is covered mostly with manzanita. That's not to say riders can't have a pleasant riding experience at Tahoe-Donner, but Northstar Stables clearly has the more impressive scenery.

Rates

The 45-minute ride is $12, the one-and-a-half-hour ride $20, and the half-day ride $50. A minimum of four people is required for the two longer rides. The breakfast ride is $20 and the dinner ride ranges from $20 to $30, depending on the choice of entree. Also, there is a sign posted near the office that states, "Tips Appreciated."

The rides at Tahoe-Donner Equestrian Center are $15 an hour.

Payment Method

Northstar Stables accepts cash, personal checks with a bank guarantee card, traveler's checks, Visa, and MasterCard.

Rider Age Limit

All riders at Northstar Stables must be at least seven years old.

How To Get There

From either Truckee to the north or Kings Beach to the south, it is a six-mile drive to Northstar along Highway 267. Look for the road signs for Northstar Drive. Follow it a short distance and look for the sign on the left for Northstar Stables. Turn up the dirt road near the sign and follow it to the end.

CASCADE STABLES

P.O. Box 7034
South Lake Tahoe, CA 96158
(916) 541-2055
Owner: H.R. Ebright

The Cascade Falls are among the most beautiful sights in the entire Lake Tahoe region. Tumbling 100 feet down a sheer granite face, they flow into serene and picturesque Cascade Lake.

Though many visitors to Lake Tahoe catch a glimpse of the falls and the lake from a distance, few ever have the opportunity to see them up close. The area has been privately owned by the same family since 1882.

The family's careful control over this priceless real estate has prevented development and has helped to keep it looking much the same as it did when Mark Twain came visiting long ago.

There is one way, however, that vacationers can enjoy all the beauty and charm of the lake and the waterfalls behind it. Cascade Stables, operated by the same family that owns the property, offers trail rides from June to October that are, by any measure, the most scenic available in the Lake Tahoe area.

Even the one-hour ride offers some pleasant scenery, although the longer rides are recommended. Leaving on the one-hour trip, riders head off through a residential area along a dirt road. Looking off through the trees to the right, they catch a view of Lake Tahoe.

A little further along, they pass active, frothy Cascade Creek as it rushes through a gauntlet of small rocks and boulders on its way to Lake Tahoe. When riders reach Highway 89 at a point just below the hairpin turn that winds around to Emerald Bay, the guide stops the traffic and the horses cross the road. Riders then proceed on to Cascade Lake. As they approach, the only development at the lake comes into view–five homes nestled in the trees near the shore that belong to the owner's family.

They then proceed along a trail that follows the shoreline around the lake. A thick forest of Douglas fir, sugar pine, ponderosa pine, and cedar extends down almost to the water's edge. This is where scenes from the motion picture *A Place in the Sun* with Elizabeth Taylor, Montgomery Cliff, and Shelley Winters were filmed.

They continue until they reach a point half way around the lake that offers an excellent view of Cascade Falls. For photographers, this is a great spot to get a snapshot. The group then turns around and heads back to the stables.

The two-hour ride starts almost the same way. But instead of turning back, riders continue around the lake along a trail engulfed in fern. The forest becomes increasingly dense as riders cross Cascade Creek just down stream from the base of the falls. Ironically, the presence of so many trees limits the view of the falls at this point. Continuing on, riders cross two more creeks and pass through an area that is particularly green and lush.

Swinging around to the other side of the lake, they continue along a trail that runs above the shoreline. It then winds away from the lake and begins to climb. Eventually it curves around to a promontory point that offers one of the most spectacular views of Lake Tahoe that vacationers will find anywhere. After feasting on all the great sights, the group heads back down the trail to Highway 89 and then on to the stables.

A promonotory overlooking Lake Tahoe

The half-day ride goes all the way to Floating Isle Lake, just inside the Desolation Wilderness boundary. The interesting feature of the lake, is that it has an island that floats. Unfortunately, careless people have broken off portions of the small island, so that today there isn't much left of it. To get to the lake, riders go up along a ridge to the south of Cascade Lake. From the trail, they can see Fallen Leaf Lake off to the left. Upon arriving at the lake, riders stop for lunch. After about a half hour at the lake, they head back down the trail to the stables. Typically, they will spend about three and a half hours in the saddle on the half-day trip.

There is an alternative for particularly hearty riders. They can ride up to Granite Lake and back. It's a steep, rough trip, but riders are rewarded with a spectacular view of Emerald Bay from the trail.

Even more ambitious riders might consider one of three alternatives for an all-day trip. They can ride down to Meeks Bay and back on one of the trips. This takes them along a trail that goes past Granite Lake, Velma Lakes, and Stony Ridge Lake. In all, it's roughly a seven-hour trip. They can also take a loop ride that stops at Velma Lakes. The third alternative is to have horses trucked over to Luther Meadow, where riders can head off to the Dardenelles.

Pack Trips

Cascade Stables also arranges extended trips. Riders can ride all the way to Tuolumne Meadows, for instance. Or horses can be trucked to Tuolumne, and they can ride back. Either way, the trip takes about 10 days. Another option is to ride to Alpine Meadows and back. That normally takes from three to four days. Trips to many other destinations within the Desolation Wilderness are also available.

Rates

The one-hour ride is $15 and the two-hour ride is $28. The half-day ride is $45 and the day-ride is $50. Cascade Stables also offers a breakfast ride for $28 and a steak ride for $30. On the extended trips, the charge is $50 per day for the horse and $100 per day for the packer. For groups of the three or more, the price for each horse is reduced to $40 per day.

Payment Method

Cascade Stables accepts cash, personal checks written on California banks, and traveler's checks.

Rider Age Limit

All riders must be at least eight years old. No doubling is permitted.

How To Get There

From South Tahoe, go north on Highway 89. From Tahoe City, go south on Highway 89. The turn for Cascade Stables is on the Lake Tahoe side of the road, just south of Emerald Bay. Follow the dirt road to the end.

CAMP RICHARDSON CORRAL

P.O. Box 8335
South Lake Tahoe, CA 96158
(916) 541-3113
Owners: Rob and Jill Ross

Back in the 1880s, it was the headquarters site of Lake Tahoe's first steam-powered railroad. In 1921, it became the main station for a popular stageline that ferried passengers around the south shore in oversized Pierce Arrows. Soon after, stageline operator Alonzo LeRoy Richardson began a major expansion. First, he built tourist cabins. Then he added a dining room, hotel, general store, gas station, and several other buildings and it became what it remains today–a rustic, lake-side resort.

It's been over 60 years now since Camp Richardson first opened in the South Lake Tahoe area and little about the place has changed. Even the old barn-red tourist cabins are in their same familiar spot. But the good news for trail riders is that Camp Richardson's long time tradition of horseback riding has continued to the present day.

Camp Richardson Corral, located immediately to the north of Camp Richardson Camp Ground, has been in business since 1934. Operating from mid-May to mid-October each year, it offers everything from one-hour trail rides to extended pack trips that travel through the area nearby.

The least-demanding rides are the one-hour trips, which can be taken along three different routes. Inexperienced riders can go out on a simple loop trail through the meadow behind Camp Richardson. Riders with more experience might consider a trip that goes through a heavy forest near Camp Richardson and up onto a knoll that overlooks Lake Tahoe. A third choice, which is normally only available either early or late in the day, is to ride over to Fallen Leaf Lake and back.

There is a better way to see Fallen Leaf Lake, however. On one of the two routes used for the two-hour trip, riders head off to the south through the meadow behind Camp Richardson. Then, as they enter the forest, they begin to climb. Eventually, they go up and over Tahoe Mountain, which sits due south of Fallen Leaf Lake at 7,249 feet elevation. At the crest of the ridge on Tahoe Mountain, they look down on three-mile-long Fallen Leaf Lake and they can glimpse a portion of Lake Tahoe off to the north. Looking to the west, they have an excellent view of 9,735 foot Mt. Tallac.

Riders drop down on the other side of Tahoe Mountain and follow a trail along the side of Fallen Leaf Lake. By approaching the lake at this point, they avoid the development at the south end. They then continue past Fallen Leaf Lake Campgrounds and back to the stables.

A second two-hour route is available for riders uncomfortable with the elevation gain on the Tahoe Mountain trip. Leaving the stables, they go up over a small hill and down past the Fallen Leaf Lake Campgrounds to Fallen Leaf Lake. They ride along the lakeshore and then swing around to follow Taylor Creek north. Along the trail back to the stables, riders pass through a grove of aspens and an open meadow.

The half-day ride goes to Floating Island Lake, just inside the Desolation Wilderness. As has been described in a previous section, the lake contains a small island that floats. At one time, it was more than twenty feet across, but over the years use and abuse have reduced its size. The trip to Floating Island Lake follows a trail along Fallen Leaf Ridge and provides excellent views of Fallen Leaf Lake and Lake Tahoe. At the lake, riders stop for lunch before returning to the stables.

Pack Trips

Camp Richardson Corral also offers spot trips and all-inclusive trips into the Desolation Wilderness. Popular overnight destinations include Lake Aloha, Stony Ridge Lake, and Upper Velma Lake. On the all-inclusive trips, meals and food preparation are included. However, riders are expected to help with the dishes and meal preparation.

Rates

The one-hour ride is $16, the two-hour ride is $32, and the half-day ride is $50. The breakfast ride is $28.50 and the steak ride is $29.50. Spot trips are $60 per day for stock and $100 per day for the packer. All-inclusive trips are $125 per day.

Payment Method

Camp Richardson Corral accepts cash, personal checks, traveler's checks, Visa, and MasterCard.

Rider Age Limit

Riders must be at least six years old.

How To Get There

From the "Y" at South Tahoe, proceed north on Highway 89. Just past Camp Richardson Campground, look for Camp Richardson Corral on the left.

STRAWBERRY CANYON STABLES

17480 Highway 50
Strawberry, CA 95720
(916) 659-7728
Owner: Lyn Chelgren

Not a whole lot has changed in Strawberry in the last hundred years. Back in the 1860s, prospectors on their way to the silver mines in Virginia City would stop at Strawberry Station for rest and refreshment. Today, it's vacationers out to strike it rich at the gaming tables in Reno and Lake Tahoe, who stop for a brief respite.

It's unfortunate that these impatient travelers can't linger in Strawberry a little longer. Because nearby there is beautiful country to explore, and an easy way to explore it. Strawberry Canyon Stables, located next to the Strawberry Lodge, at an elevation of 5,800 feet, offers trail rides of various lengths throughout the year.

The one-hour ride is the one best suited for beginners. It starts with riders heading out the front gate, and along Highway 50 past Strawberry Lodge. They then swing right and go across the American River, which runs behind the lodge. They circle a neighborhood of summer cabins nestled amid the aspen and pine, before heading up a trail that is lined with granite boulders and rock outcroppings.

During the first 15 minutes of the trip, riders have an excellent view of Lover's Leap, a large granite promontory that rises from the canyon floor. Continuing up the trail, they reach a ridge that offers scenic views up the American River Canyon. Farther along, they skirt Strawberry Creek and beautiful Strawberry Meadow. After passing the junction with 42 Mile Road, they loop back to the stables.

The two-hour trip is intended for more experienced riders. It follows the same route as the one-hour ride until it reaches Strawberry Creek. Instead of skirting the creek, riders on this trip cross the creek and continue up Strawberry Canyon. Along the way, there are stretches on an old logging road where those with the experience and ability can break into a lope.

There is more elevation gain on the two-hour trip and better panoramas. Looking across to the north, riders can spot Pyramid Peak, located in the Desolation Wilderness. Eventually, the trail loops back down to the stables.

For those eager to get a closer look at Lover's Leap, the three-hour ride goes right up to the top. The first half of the trip is a steady climb and the return trip is all downhill. But up on top of Lover's Leap, at over 7,000 feet in elevation, it levels out enough for riders to enjoy a sweeping view all up and down the canyon.

The most ambitious trip, however, and in many ways the most scenic, takes a half day. Following an old logging road, riders head south. They make a few stream crossings and travel alongside Cody Creek. Along the way, they sometimes encounter deer, bear, coyote, and even the occasional porcupine.

Eventually they reach a saddle and then drop down to Cody Lake, which sits at 8,000 feet in elevation. At one end of the lake is a beautiful meadow filled with lupines, snow plants, and Indian paint brush. At the other end, there are a series of boulders that surround an excellent spot for swimming.

Riders stop for lunch by the lake, and sometimes go for a swim. Among the sights they can see from the lake are Pyramid Peak, Horsetail Falls, and Lover's Leap down below. After enjoying the pleasant mountain scenery, the group heads back down to the stables.

During the wintertime, vacationers can go horseback riding through a snow-covered forest, weather permitting. But the shorter trips are recommended, because it can get quite cold.

Rates

Rides are $15.00 for the first hour and $10.00 for each additional hour. On rides over four hours long, the rate is a flat $10.00 per hour.

Payment Method

Strawberry Canyon Stables accepts cash, personal checks, and traveler's checks.

Rider Age Limit

There is no specific limit, but the owner will not permit anyone to ride who is considered incapable. Doubles are permitted.

How To Get There

Traveling east on Highway 50, Strawberry is the first stop after Kyburz. Look for the stables on the right as you enter Strawberry. The entrance is just west of the Strawberry Lodge.

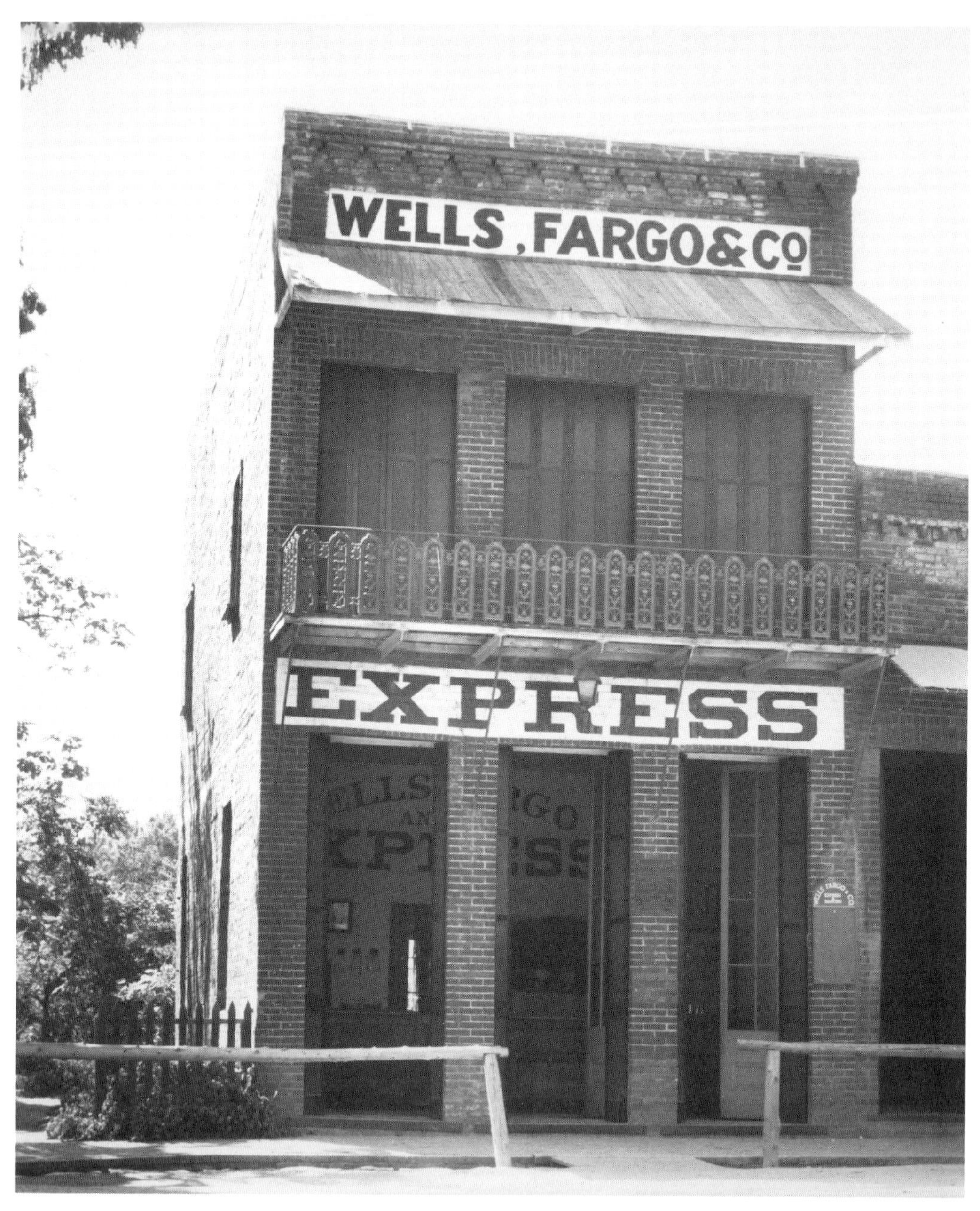

Main Street in Columbia Historic State Park

MOTHER LODE AND SONORA PASS 5

COLUMBIA RIDING STABLE

P.O. Box 1777
Columbia, CA 95310
(209) 532-0663
Owners: Gary and Davy Stoller

There's no telling what course the history of California might have taken, had James W. Marshall not stumbled onto gold that fateful January day back in 1848. But once the word spread, the wild, the adventurous, and the unabashedly greedy grabbed any available means of transportation and came swarming into California by the thousands.

One of the many cities that the fortune seekers descended on was Columbia, then known as Hildreth's Diggin's, near Sonora in the heart of the Mother Lode. Virtually overnight in the early 1850s, Columbia grew to a population of over 5,000 people as tents and shanties sprang up everywhere. By 1860, the population had declined to only 500 and Columbia became yet another virtual ghost town.

Fortunately, however, a number of the buildings from the once-thriving mining town remained largely intact, and in 1945 the Columbia State Historic Park was created.

Columbia Riding Stable, headquartered inside the park, offers trail rides from 15 minutes to four hours in length that go around the park and beyond.

The rides, available daily from Memorial Day through Labor Day, and on weekends and holidays the rest of the year, are divided into two groups – beginning and experienced. The shortest of the beginner rides, the 15-minute trip, is really intended for small children who just want to get up on a horse. It ventures only a short distance from the stable and would probably not satisfy anyone older.

The half-hour beginner ride appeals to a broader age range. From the stable, riders head up along a trail that passes through a landscape typical of the Sierra foothill region. Crossing the dirt road used for stage rides, riders climb up through a limestone canyon to a marble quarry and then return.

On the one-hour beginner trip, riders venture up into the hydraulic mining area, but then on their return, they swing over to the town's old school house located by the graveyard. Both the school house and the graveyard are frequently missed by visitors to Columbia.

The two-story, red brick school house, in particular, is noteworthy because it is so well preserved. One of the first public schools in California, it continued to operate until 1937.

Riders complete the trip with a ride down historical Main Street, past the covered walks and classic old brick buildings. For kids, in particular, it's a movie fantasy come true as they ride past the still-operating blacksmith shop, the old newspaper office, and the restored Wells Fargo Express Building.

The two-hour ride for beginners goes to a different area of the park, away from the historical buildings, to a place known as the 80 acres. Once there, riders travel through a big meadow and then up into the nearby hills. At the highest point, riders can look down on the city below or off in the direction of Yosemite. They return to the stable the way they came.

More experienced riders have five different trips to choose from. The shortest is 45 minutes long and is similar to the beginners' half-hour ride, except that it goes up to an overlook above the hydraulic mining area. From the overlook, riders have an excellent view of the city of Columbia. At that point, they turn around.

On the one-hour trip, they begin along the 45-minute route and then continue on to the other side of the mountain to view yet another hydraulic mining area. Along the way, they enter a forest of manzanita and pass through a manzanita tunnel. On their return trip, if time permits, they go past Saint Anne's Catholic Church. Completed in 1857, it is one of the oldest brick churches in California.

The 90-minute ride is simply a variation on the one-hour trip. On the 90-minute trip, instead of going by Saint Anne's Catholic Church, riders go by the school house and then down Main Street for the last leg of the ride.

There are two alternatives for the two-hour trip. Riders can either follow the same route out to the 80 acres that is taken by the beginners or they can ride over to a lush, green field near the Springfield Trout Farm. At either spot, riders have an opportunity to lope, though the Springfield location is probably the preferable place for this. The 80 acres is the better choice for good views.

The ultimate ride offered by Columbia Riding Stable, though, is the four-hour trip. Basically, it is all the other rides combined. Riders go up to the hydraulic mining area, down through town, over to the 80 acres, and across to Springfield. For those who have the time, it's a great way to see the park and surrounding area. It also offers ample opportunities for loping.

One tip for those planning a trip to Columbia – avoid the middle of the summer. The temperature on a typical August day is between 90° and 100°. The best time to come is in the springtime.

Rates

The 15-minute beginner ride is $6 and the 30-minute beginner ride is $10. The one-hour beginner ride is $18 and the two-hour beginner ride is $32. The 45-minute experienced ride is $14 and the one-hour experienced ride is $18. The 90-minute experience ride is $25 and the two-hour experienced ride is $32. The four-hour experienced ride is $55. Reservations are required for the four-hour ride and there must be a minimum group of four people.

Method Of Payment

Columbia Riding Stable accepts cash, personal checks, traveler's checks, Visa, and MasterCard.

Rider Age Limit

There is no minimum age limit. Children four and under may double with a parent.

How To Get There

From Sonora, take Highway 49 north. At Columbia State Historic Park, enter the first parking lot on the right and go to the end. Columbia Riding Stable is at the end of the parking lot.

RENO SARDELLA'S PACK STATION

P.O. Box 1435
Pinecrest, CA 95364
(209) 965-3402 (Summer)
(209) 984-5727 (Winter)
(209) 984-5452 (Winter)
Manager: LaVerne Litteral

For centuries, people have been coming to the forests and meadows around Pinecrest in the western Sierra Nevada. The earliest visitors were the Miwok Indians, who came up from lower elevations each summer to forage, hunt, and trade with other tribes. In the 1850s, wagon loads of emigrants passed through the area on their way to the gold fields of the Mother Lode. Following soon after were the sheep herders , who brought their flocks to graze the meadows around Pinecrest.

These days, the area attracts invaders of another kind. In the winter, skiers head to the slopes at Dodge Ridge. While in the summer, vacationers go boating on Pinecrest Lake, and hiking, fishing, and camping in the nearby Emigrant Wilderness. Of course, there's one other way for vacationers to spend their time in Pinecrest. They can head to a nearby stables for a ride through this scenic area on a horse.

A young wrangler from Reno Sardella's Pack Station

Reno Sardella's Pack Station, only a short drive from Pinecrest Lake and just over the hill from Dodge Ridge Ski Area, offers trail rides of various lengths in and around the surrounding region.

The most popular of these is the one-hour ride. Following a trail through a forest of fir and pine, riders are treated to a number of panoramic high Sierra views. Perched on the side of ridge, for instance, they can look down on Bell Meadow and out across the wilderness all the way to Yosemite National Park. From certain spots, they even catch views of 10,015 foot high Haystack Peak inside the park boundaries.

Along the way, they travel through mountain meadows and past the kinds of granite outcroppings so common in this part of the Sierra.

Eventually, they work their way back down to the pack station, sitting in Aspen Meadow.

On the half-day trip, riders depart along the same trail, but then swing over to the upper end of Crabtree Meadow. They continue on through heavily forested Pine Valley and down into Bell Meadow, grazing land for cattle and horses, before returning to the pack station.

More experienced riders, however, may prefer the all-day trip, which actually ventures inside the Emigrant Wilderness. Proceeding along a trail that passes the few remaining logs of what was once Gianelli Cabin, riders reach the wilderness boundary at Burst Rock. Continuing, they travel to Powell Lake, sitting resplendently in a granite bowl, and then over to Chewing Gum Lake. Surrounded by large rock ledges and stands of lodgepole pine, the scenic mountain lake provides a pleasant setting for lunch. After relaxing at the lake and enjoying sweeping backcountry vistas, riders return to the pack station along a trail that passes through Crabtree Camp.

As an alternative, riders can also take all-day trips to either Bear Lake or Grouse Lake for fishing, swimming, or unwinding.

Pack Station

Most of the overnight trips offered by Reno Sardella's are spot trips, though extended trips are available as well. They can be arranged to virtually any destination within the 118,000 acre Emigrant Wilderness for however many days a rider desires.

Rates

The one-hour ride is $15 and the half-day ride is $37. The all-day ride is $45. For spot and extended trips, a packer with horse is $95 per day and saddle and pack animals are $40 per day.

Method Of Payment

Reno Sardella's Pack Station accepts cash, personal checks, and traveler's checks.

Rider Age Limit

There is no set age limit, however, the pack station will make judgement calls about individual riders.

How To Get There

From Sonora, take Highway 108 east. At Pinecrest, take the turn-off to Dodge Ridge Ski Area. Turn onto Crabtree Road and look for the pack station sign.

KENNEDY MEADOWS PACK STATION

Star Route, Box 1490
Sonora, CA 95370
(209) 965-3900 (Summer)
(209) 532-9096 (Winter)
Owner: Willie Ritts

Back in 1841, seven years before the discovery of gold in California, 60 members of the Bartleson/Bidwell Party became the first pioneers to successfully conquer the Sierra Nevada along a route over the Emigrant Pass.

As gold fever spread in the 1850s, wagons began making the climb over the Sierra Nevada through this region just north of Yosemite National Park on a regular basis. Eventually, it became known as a leading entryway for emigrants to California and the name "Emigrant" became attached to it.

Today, little has changed about the 118,000-acre area now known as the Emigrant Wilderness, and it has become a great place for hiking, fishing, and camping. Best of all, it has become a great place to ride a horse. Kennedy Meadows Pack Station, located a few miles below the Sonora Pass, offers half-day and all-day rides as well as extended journeys that travel through the Emigrant Wilderness.

The pack station, open from early April through mid October each year, also offers a one-and-a-quarter-hour ride at 10:00 a.m., 12:00 noon, 2:00 p.m., and 4:00 p.m. that stays within the immediate Kennedy Meadows area. On this easy-going loop through the woods, riders follow the Middle Fork Stanislaus River as it winds through the Kennedy Meadows Resort. The resort, in operation since 1886, consists of a series of rustic cabins, a restaurant, a bar, and a general store.

At the first bridge upstream, riders cross over the river and travel through the upper meadow. Then they swing down along the far shore of the river and head south. Eventually, they cross back over by fording the river and return to the pack station. It's a pleasant trip and quite scenic for a ride of this length.

On the half-day trip, which departs at 9:30 a.m. and 1:30 p.m., riders head off along a trail that follows the Middle Fork Stanislaus up towards the Relief Reservoir. They travel through Kennedy Meadow, named for an early cattle rancher, and past a dramatic display of granite that served as the backdrop for a scene from the movie *Mail Order Bride.* Eventually, they reach the reservoir, created by the Pacific Gas & Electric Company back in 1921, and then continue around to a point near where Grouse Creek flows into the reservoir.

The riders dismount for a half-hour break at this spot right on the border of the Emigrant Wilderness. Looking off to the southeast, they have an excellent view of the scenic wilderness area, with 10,808 foot high Relief Peak standing out as the most prominent feature. After their break, they return to the pack station.

Even more spectacular scenery is available on the all-day trip to Kennedy Lake. Riders catch views of Granite Dome and East Flange Rock as they work their way up the Kennedy Creek Trail. At one point, they cross roaring Kennedy Creek as they continue following it upstream. The vegetation varies as they travel, with stretches of Jeffrey pine and juniper, replaced by open expanses of sagebrush, only to be replaced by thick forests of lodgepole pine.

Riders pass Soda Canyon as they approach Kennedy Lake. Sitting above 8,000 feet in elevation, the lake is surrounded by a wide meadow, with 10,716 foot high Kennedy Peak looming above. The group stops for lunch and the fishermen in the group get a chance to try their luck with the rainbow and brown trout in the lake. After everyone has time to thoroughly relax, they all saddle up and head back down the trail.

Pack Trips

Kennedy Meadows Pack Station arranges both extended and spot trips, though most of their business is in spot trips. Popular destinations include Huckleberry Lake, Emigrant Lake, Upper Buck, Lower Buck, Long Lake, and Deer Lake. For those interested in an extended trip, one to consider might be the four-day trip to Tuolumne Meadows by way of Bond Pass.

Rates

The one-and-a-quarter-hour ride is $15. The half-day ride is $35 and the all-day ride is $45. For spot trips and extended trips, a packer with horse is $90. Saddle horses and pack animals are $35 per day for trips up to eight miles and $40 per day for trips over eight miles. For trips eight days or longer, the charge is $32.50 per day. All pack rates are $5 higher in the fall.

Payment Method

Kennedy Meadows Pack Station accepts cash, personal checks, and traveler's checks.

Rider Age Limit

All riders must be at least six years old.

How To Get There

From Sonora, take Highway 108 east. Go approximately 58 miles and look for the turn-off to Kennedy Meadows Resort on the right. Follow the road into the resort and look for the pack station behind the store.

Covered bridge at the Pioneer Yosemite History Center in Wawona

YOSEMITE 6

MATHER PACK STATION

Camp Mather, CA
(Winter Address)
12942 Highway 120
Oakdale, CA 95361
(209) 847-5753 (W)
(209) 379-2334 (S)
Owner: Jay Barnes

It's hard to imagine there could be another valley on the face of the earth as awe-inspiring as Yosemite Valley in Yosemite National Park. For those who have had the opportunity to see it, the Hetch Hetchy Valley in the northwest corner of the park is every bit as beautiful. Regrettably, no one will ever see it again, because it's now under water.

In 1913, over the impassioned objections of conservationist John Muir, it was decided that the magnificent Hetch Hetchy Valley would become the site of a reservoir for the city of San Francisco.

Today, vacationers visit Hetch Hetchy primarily to discover what is left of the once scenic valley and to imagine what might have been.

Mather Pack Station, located in nearby Camp Mather a mile outside the national park boundary, offers several trail rides, including one that provides excellent views of the Hetch Hetchy Reservoir. Open from early June through Labor Day, the pack station primarily serves guests of Camp Mather, a 360-acre resort owned by the city of San Francisco. But anyone interested in a trail ride is welcome.

The trip to the Hetch Hetchy overlook, a two-hour ride, leaves every day at 9:00 a.m. Taking off through a forest of fir and pine, riders head up into Yosemite National Park. As they travel, they make a steep climb through a rocky area known as the Golden Stairs. Eventually, they reach a granite dome that offers a panoramic view of the canyon below.

Looking off to the northeast, riders can see O'Shaughnessy Dam and the Hetch Hetchy Reservoir. After enjoying the view, the group returns to the pack station.

There are, of course, several other rides available as well. Four times a day – 9:00 a.m., 10:00 a.m., 2:00 p.m., 4:00 p.m. – Mather Pack Station conducts one-hour rides that loop through the forest near Camp Mather. Along the way, riders pass through a mountain meadow. Though there are no noteworthy sights during the trip, riders can have an enjoyable time on a horse.

At 2:00 p.m. each day, the pack station offers a two-hour ride that is essentially an extended version of the trip just described. Later, at 6:30, there's a 90-minute sunset ride.

Vacationers interested in fishing or swimming might consider the half-day ride. Departing at 1:00 p.m. each afternoon, the trip goes over to Middlefork Creek. After riding for about an hour, the group reaches the creek, where they can fish, swim, snooze, or read a book. Generally, the group gets back to the pack station around 5:00 p.m.

The most scenic trip offered by Mather Pack Station, however, is the all-day ride to Smith Peak. On this trip, riders hit the trail at 8:30 a.m. along the same route taken for the Hetch Hetchy overlook ride. Part way up the trail, they then take a fork off to the right and continue on to Smith Peak. About 250 feet from the top, riders dismount and complete the journey up the steep trail on foot.

For their efforts, they are well rewarded. On top of 7,751 foot high Smith Peak, they have a 360° view of the surrounding region, including the Sierra Crest. They also have a birds-eye view of the Grand Canyon of the Tuolumne River and of the backend of the Hetch Hetchy Reservoir 4,000 feet below. Back at Smith Meadow, at the base of the peak, riders stop for lunch. Then they travel back to the pack station, arriving around 4:30 p.m.

Mather Pack Station also offers breakfast and dinner rides to a grassy meadow about an hour's riding time from the pack station. On the breakfast ride, which goes from 8:00 a.m. to 11:00 a.m., riders are served scrambled eggs, bacon, fried potatoes, biscuits, and fruit. For the dinner ride, which goes from 4:00 p.m. to 7:00 p.m., the group is served steak, corn-on-the-cob, beans, French bread, and salad. After each of the meals, the group goes down into China Gulch and around Mud Lake.

Pack Trips

Mather Pack Station specializes in spot trips into the northwestern section of Yosemite National Park. Some of the popular destinations for a one-day trip are Beehive Meadow, Laurel Lake, Rancheria Falls, and Vernon Falls. Some of the two-day destinations include Paradise Valley, Wilmer Lake, Pleasant Valley, and Miwok Lake. Extended trips through these areas are also available.

Rates

One-hour rides are $15, and 90-minute rides are $18. Two-hour rides are $20 and half-day rides are $25. The all-day trip to Smith Peak is $35. Both the breakfast and dinner rides are $25. Saddle and pack horses are $40 per day. A packer with horse is $90 per day.

Payment Method

Mather Pack Station accepts cash, personal checks, and traveler's checks.

Rider Age Limit

All riders must be at least seven years old.

How To Get There

From Highway 120, take the turn-off to Hetch Hetchy just before the Big Oak Flat Entrance to Yosemite National Park. Continue to Camp Mather. Look for the pack station just beyond Camp Mather on the right.

WHITE WOLF STABLES

Yosemite National Park, CA 95389
(209) 375-1323
Owner: Yosemite Park and Curry Co.

For centuries, it had been a summer camp for a tribe of Indians. Flat, grassy and surrounded by lodgepole pines, it was as peaceful as it was isolated, until one day in the early 1870s, John Meyer stumbled upon it by accident. Surveying this meadow filled with wildflowers near the Middle Fork Tuolumne River, he realized it would be ideal for grazing cattle. Soon after, he set out to homestead it for himself.

In honor of the Indian chief he effectively displaced, he named the homestead White Wolf. Over the years, the Meyer family transformed the cattle ranch into a guest lodge and eventually it was sold to the park service. Today, White Wolf Lodge continues to accommodate guests, who come to hike, fish, or camp in the northwest corner of the park.

It also accommodates visitors who would like to ride a horse. White Wolf Stables, open from June through Labor Day each year, offers two-hour, half-day, and all-day rides around the immediate area. Offering more intimate rides than are found elsewhere in the park, White Wolf generally limits the number of riders on each trip to six.

On the two-hour trip, riders can either go to Lukens Lake or Harden Lake. Both are about equal distance from the stables, however, the trail to Lukens Lake is more heavily forested with lodgepole pine. Beginners will find the ride to Harden Lake to be the easier of the two.

Neither of the two-hour rides, however, offer scenery comparable to what is found on the half-day trips. On the first of the two trips, riders head down the trail towards Lukens Lake, but then cut off through Harden's Gardens. As its name suggests, there is an abundance of plant life and brightly-colored wildflowers in Harden's Gardens.

After enjoying the scenic floral display, riders travel through a forest of sugar pine and past stands of aspen as they head over to Harden Lake. From the lake, they return along the two-hour trail to the stables.

As an alternative, riders might consider the half-day trip to an overlook above the Grand Canyon of the Tuolumne. Regarded by many as one of the most scenic spots in all of Yosemite National Park, the deep, glacier-carved gorge is rarely seen by visitors. Upon reaching the overlook, riders have from 15 to 20 minutes to take in the whole panoramic view of this spectacular canyon. They can even trace the path of the Tuolumne River as it flows through the canyon into the Hetch Hetchy Reservoir behind O'Shaughnessy Dam. From the overlook, they return to the stables.

More ambitious riders might consider an all-day trip that combines the two half-day rides. They travel to Lukens Lake, through Harden's Gardens, before heading out to the overlook above the Grand Canyon of the Sierra.

For something completely different, they can take the all-day trip to Ten Lakes. It's a rough trip with numerous switchbacks and is recommended for experienced riders only. For those with the stamina, however, the series of alpine lakes are quite scenic and the trip over and back provides riders with a true taste of the backcountry.

Pack Trips

White Wolf Stables also offers spot and extended trips. Among the suggested destinations for spot trips are Ten Lakes, Grant Lakes, Pate Valley, and Rodgers Lake. A suggested six-day, five-night extended trip makes stops at Pate Valley, Return Creek, Glen Aulin, South fork of Cathedral Creek, and Ten Lakes.

Rates

The two-hour ride is $28 and the half-day ride is $38. The all-day ride is $58. For spot and extended trips, a packer is $110 per day. Pack and saddle animals are $59 per day.

Payment Method

White Wolf Stables accepts cash, personal checks, traveler's checks, MasterCard, Visa, Diners Club, Discover, and American Express.

Rider Age Limit

Riders must be at least seven years old. Children 12 and under must wear helmets. Helmets are also available for all other riders.

How To Get There

From Highway 99, take Highway 140 east from Merced. Continue on past Mariposa to Yosemite National Park. From the entrance, proceed to the Tuolumne Meadows turnoff. Take Highway 108 towards Tuolumne Meadows. Look for the White Wolf turnoff, approximately 14 miles past Crane Flat. Take the road into White Wolf and look for the stables behind the lodge.

TUOLUMNE MEADOWS STABLES

Yosemite National Park, CA 95389
(209) 372-1327
Owner: Yosemite Park and Curry Co.

The last glacier disappeared from what is now Tuolumne Meadows many years ago. But the signs of its impact remain in evidence even today. Smoothly-polished granite domes and dramatically-sculpted mountain peaks surround this high country meadow.

The meadow itself, sitting at 8,600 feet in elevation, is a direct byproduct of the glacier. After evolving from an ice field to a lake and then to grassland, Tuolumne Meadows is, today, the largest subalpine meadow in the Sierra Nevada range. It is also one of the most beautiful.

Tuolumne Meadows Stables, open from June through September each year, offers trail rides to many of the most scenic spots in the region. There are two-hour, half-day, and all-day rides, as well as custom overnight trips.

For those with limited time or experience, the two-hour ride serves as a pleasant introduction to Tuolumne Meadows. Departing at 8:00 a.m., 10:00 a.m., 1:00 p.m., and 3:00 p.m., riders head off along a trail that winds through the lodgepole pines that ring the meadow. During the month of July, the grassy expanse is covered with a blanket of colorful wild flowers, including Lemmon's Paintbrush.

Looking across Tuolumne Meadows, riders also catch views of Unicorn Peak, Cathedral Peak, and Echo Peaks. Continuing along the trail, they ford two creeks and travel across wide, polished slabs of granite. Eventually, they reach their turn-around point near the roaring Tuolumne River. On the way back, the group follows a different route that takes them down near Soda Springs, before making the last gentle climb to the stables.

Vacationers have two choices for the half-day trip. They can either ride over to Tuolumne Falls or up to Elizabeth Lake. The Elizabeth Lake trip, however, is only recommended for more experienced riders and should be avoided early in the season because of a mosquito problem. Both trips depart either at 8:00 a.m. or 1:00 p.m.

Tuolumne Meadows

Along the way, they go past Little Devil's Postpile, a small, plug-like lava formation that is unique within the Yosemite National Park boundaries. Continuing toward the falls, they pass stretches of white water, with alternating, quieter pools.

At the falls, riders are treated to a display of gushing, cascading water that varies in intensity depending upon the time of year. On the return trip, they have an excellent view of the Cathedral Range.

For the alternative half-day trip to Elizabeth Lake, riders head out across Tuolumne Meadows and then climb through a forest of lodgepole pine, crossing occasional streams as they go.

Eventually, they reach what is regarded as one of the most beautiful lakes in the Tuolumne Meadows region. Surrounded by a lush, green meadow, with glacier-carved Unicorn Peak rising up behind it, this enchanting lake just begs to be photographed. After enjoying the sights and taking pictures, riders turn around and head back to the stables.

More ambitious riders may prefer the all-day trips. Offered by advance reservation and only for groups of at least three people, the all-day trips use saddle mules rather than horses because of the treacherous terrain. Vacationers can choose to go to either Water Wheel Falls, Vogelsang High Sierra Camp, or Cathedral Lake. The latter two are interesting throughout the summer. Water Wheel Falls, however, is best enjoyed early in the season, while the water levels are still high.

On the Water Wheel Falls trip, riders follow the trail down to Tuolumne Falls and then continue on to Glen Aulin High Sierra Camp, where they view frothy White Cascades. They follow the Tuolumne River further downstream, passing California Falls and La Conte Falls, before reaching Water Wheel Falls

In the truest sense of the word, Water Wheel is not a fall at all. Rather it is a steep cascade through a series of rock ledges that kick the water up as high as 30 or 40 feet into the air. The effect is quite spectacular, made even more so, if the sun catches the mist just right, creating a colorful rainbow. By August, however, the show is essentially over.

Those visiting the area later in the season might prefer the trip to Vogelsang. Departing from Tuolumne Meadows, riders slowly work their way up through lodgepole pine forests and wildflower-festooned meadows to a point above the treeline. Continuing through the glacier-scrubbed, boulder-strewn terrain, riders catch views of the nearby snowcapped peaks.

Eventually, they reach Vogelsang, sitting at the south end of Fletcher Lake, where everyone dismounts for an hour and a half stopover before heading back down to the stables.

The third alternative is to ride to upper Cathedral Lake. For this trip, riders head off on the John Muir Trail, the most popular route between Tuolumne Meadows and Yosemite Valley. They travel past Fairview Dome and then up through a series of switchbacks.

Eventually, they reach the picturesque lake, with jagged Cathedral Peak rising up above it. The peak is particularly distinctive, because it was never touched by the glaciers that passed through the area and so it lacks the smooth, polished surface so common in Yosemite. At the lake, riders have between 45 minutes and an hour and a half to eat lunch and do some hiking. Then they head back down to Tuolumne Meadows.

High Camp Trips

Many people may have heard of Yosemite's famous High Sierra Camps, which provide overnight food and lodging in remote spots in the back country. What they may not know is that it's possible to travel to the different camps by horseback. Tuolumne Meadows Stables offers four-day and six-day all-inclusive High Sierra Camp trips, beginning the last week in June and continuing through Labor Day each year.

With saddle mules as their trusty mounts, riders travel to a different camp each day and stay in tent cabins featuring clean linens, hot showers, and bathrooms. Hot, hearty meals are included. All riders need are a few changes of clothes and some basic toiletry items.

The four-day trips depart on Tuesdays and Fridays. On the Tuesday trips, riders travel to Glen Aulin, May Lake and Sunrise Camps and on the Friday trips they go to Vogelsang, Merced Lake and Sunrise Camps.

Six-day trips depart on Saturdays, Sundays and Wednesdays and travel to Glen Aulin, May Lake, Sunrise, Merced Lake, and Vogelsang Camps.

As might be expected, these trips are extremely popular, so reservations should be made well in advance. Tuolumne Meadows Stables does not handle the reservations, however. Instead, interested people should call (209) 454-2002 for information and reservations.

Pack Trips

Tuolumne Meadows Stables also offers spot and extended trips. Among the suggested destinations for spot trips are Young Lake, Lower Lyell Base Camp, Ireland Lake, and Evelyn Lake. A suggested eight-day, seven-night extended trip makes stops at Virginia Canyon, Matterhorn Canyon, Smedberg Lake, Rodgers Lake, Pate Valley, Return Creek, and Glen Aulin.

Rates

The two-hour ride is $28 and the half-day ride is $38. The all-day ride is $58. Four-day High Sierra Camp trips are $478.64 for adults and $429.95 for children. Six-day High Sierra Camp trips are $754.40 for adults and $673.25 for children. For spot and extended trips, a packer is $110 per day. Pack and saddle animals are $59 per day.

Payment Method

Tuolumne Meadows Stables accepts cash, personal checks, traveler's checks, MasterCard, Visa, Diners Club, Discover, and American Express.

Rider Age Limit

Riders must be at least seven years old. Children 12 and under must wear helmets. Helmets are also available for all other riders. For the High Sierra Camp trips, riders under 12 must have had previous riding experience.

How To Get There

From Highway 99, take Highway 140 east from Merced. Continue on past Mariposa to Yosemite National Park. From the entrance, proceed to the Tuolumne Meadows turnoff. Take Highway 108 to Tuolumne Meadows. Look for the turnoff on the left, just past the Tuolumne Meadows Visitors Center. Follow the road up to the stables.

YOSEMITE VALLEY STABLES

Yosemite National Park, CA 95389
(209) 372-1248
Owner: Yosemite Park and Curry Co.

For centuries, it went all but undiscovered, its remarkable beauty known only to a few. Then, on March 27, 1851, a band of soldiers in the Mariposa Battalion stumbled upon it, and gave the valley its name–Yosemite. Soon the word spread and within four years the first organized party of tourists visited by horseback.

Today, despite heavy usage and expanded development on the valley floor, the surrounding landscape remains essentially unchanged. With its massive walls of carved and polished granite and its exquisite waterfalls, Yosemite Valley is one of the great wonders of the world.

It also continues to be a great place to sightsee by horseback. Yosemite Valley Stables, headquarters of the largest horse rental operation in the world, offers trail rides to many of the valley's most scenic spots from mid-March through late November each year. Of course, the rides are not as intimate as one might find elsewhere, with groups sometimes containing as many as 25 people. But they are professionally managed and expertly led.

The shortest of the rides, the two-hour trip, leaves with a frequency that many airlines might envy–every hour on the hour from 8:00 a.m. to 4:00 p.m. Only the first ride of the day, however, goes to Yosemite Falls. After that, the area around the falls becomes too congested and the other trips during the day follow a totally different route.

On the 8:00 a.m. trip, riders have an opportunity to travel from the stables, which sit in the shadow of Half Dome, out towards the western end of the valley. They pass through flower-dotted meadows and have an opportunity to observe the remarkable range of plant life that flourishes in the park. Eventually, they wind around through the trees to the base of lower Yosemite Falls.

From the falls, riders begin the trip back. They travel past the Church Bowl Amphitheater, the Ahwahnee Hotel, and Royal Arches. Then, as they complete the final leg of the journey, they gaze at the glacier-sculpted, 4,748-foot vertical face of Half Dome rising up before them. That just might be the most awe-inspiring view of the whole ride.

The other two-hour rides go up into the Mirror Meadow area of Tenaya Canyon. Traveling through what once was Mirror Lake, riders are able to observe how a lake can slowly transform into a meadow as part of a natural and inevitable process. Ultimately, of course, Mirror Meadow will be replaced by a forest and the cycle will be complete.

While out on the trail, riders have an opportunity to view Half Dome from three different angles and to catch a glimpse of Illilouette

Fall. They also pass near Washington Column, the most popular rock climbing spot in the valley, and ride through the Indian Caves area. Eventually, the trail loops back around to the stables.

On the half-day trips, riders travel by saddle mule rather than on horseback, because of the steep terrain. Departing at 8:00 a.m. and 1:00 p.m. each day, riders head off along a trail that goes up past Happy Isles and follows the Merced River upstream.

After a steep, 2,000 foot ascent, they reach Clark Point, half way between Vernal and Nevada Falls, and everyone dismounts for a 20 to 30 minute rest. Looking up Merced Canyon, riders have a spectacular view of powerful Nevada Falls, as its great mass of frothing, churning water comes crashing down on the rocks below.

From Clark Point, riders work their way down to Vernal Falls, where they again dismount for 20 to 30 minutes of sightseeing. During the stop, riders have an opportunity to use a rest room. They're also treated to more exceptional photo opportunities as they look out on Vernal Falls.

On the way back down the trail, riders are treated to views of Illilouette Fall, Glacier Point, Liberty Cap, 9,926 foot high Clouds Rest, and off in the distance, Yosemite Falls.

For the most complete look at Yosemite Valley, however, vacationers might consider one of the all-day trips. Departing every day, except Wednesday, at 8:00 a.m., the all-day trips also use saddle mules. On Tuesdays, Thursdays, and Sundays, the all-day ride goes up to the base of Half Dome, while on Mondays, Thursdays, and Saturdays it goes up to Glacier Point.

The all-day trip to Half Dome begins along the same route as the half-day ride. Near Vernal Falls, riders swing over onto the famous John Muir Trail and continue up to Clark Point and then on past Nevada Falls. They travel through the Little Yosemite Valley over to the base of Half Dome.

Generally, they arrive at Half Dome between 11:30 and 11:45 a.m. and everyone dismounts for the climb to the top. Only those in excellent physical condition and comfortable with heights, however, should consider the climb. It's a tough, demanding ascent up a ladder constructed out of cable and anyone with a fear of heights will end up with their heart in their stomach.

For those who make the 40-minute climb, the experience is quite exhilarating. Surprisingly, however, the view from the top, though good, isn't as exceptional as one might expect. Riders get a better opportunity for picture taking, when they stop at Nevada Falls on the way back.

The best opportunities for unforgettable pictures, however, occur on the all-day trip to Glacier Point. It offers a greater range of scenery and more chances to see the many sights and landmarks in the valley than is possible virtually any other way. As with the Half Dome trip, riders first climb the trail up to Nevada Falls. After a brief stop at the falls, they turn off onto the Panorama Trail and continue on to Illilouette Fall, where they take another short break.

They then begin the ascent of Glacier Point through a series of switchbacks, eventually reaching the top. At Glacier Point, everyone dismounts for a lengthy visit. Riders can tour the geological exhibit, grab a bite to eat at the snack bar, and go out on the point to enjoy what many consider the most breathtaking view in Yosemite.

After lunch and relaxation, riders continue west, before descending the rugged Four-Mile Trail. It takes about two hours to make it down to the valley floor, but along the way riders are treated to exceptional views of the entire western end of the valley. They can see the meadows, the dramatic granite formations, and, of course, Yosemite Falls.

Once back on the valley floor, they travel through the meadows, past the chapel, and behind Curry Village, before winding their way back to the stables. It makes for a very full day, but one that's hard to ever forget.

Pack Trips

Yosemite Valley Stables also offers spot and extended trips. Among the suggested destinations for spot trips are Merced Lake, Washburn Lake, and Ottoway Lake. A suggested five-day, four-night extended trip makes stops at Washburn Lake, Harriet Lake, Merced Peak, and Ottoway Lake.

Rates

The two-hour ride is $28 and the half-day ride is $38. The all-day ride is $58. For spot and extended trips, a packer is $110 per day. Pack and saddle animals are $59 per day.

Payment Method

Yosemite Valley Stables accepts cash, personal checks, traveler's checks, MasterCard, Visa, Diners Club, Discover, and American Express.

Rider Age Limit

Riders must be at least seven years old. Children 12 and under must wear helmets. Helmets are also available for all other riders.

How To Get There

From Highway 99, take Highway 140 east from Merced. Continue on past Mariposa to Yosemite National Park. From the entrance, proceed into the valley and take Southside Drive. The stable is located at the end of Southside Drive.

WAWONA STABLES

Yosemite National Park, CA 95389
(209) 375-6502
Owner: Yosemite Park and Curry Co.

There are no 3,000 foot high walls of granite here or dramatic spires and peaks. Even the giant sequoias of the Mariposa Grove are several miles away. But what Wawona, a rest stop for weary travelers since the 1850s, does offer is an absence of crowds and an easy going pace.

Even its centerpiece, the Wawona Hotel, has a certain old-world refinement and charm. It's hard to imagine traffic jams, long lines, or even loud arguments here.

It's also an enjoyable place to go for a ride on a horse. Wawona Stables, located only a short distance from the hotel, offers rides around the Wawona area from June through mid-September each year.

As is standard with all the stables in Yosemite National Park, there are three basic trips: a two-hour ride, a half-day ride, and an all-day ride. But, unlike Yosemite Valley Stables, there are never more than 12 riders in a group at Wawona.

On the two-hour trip, riders depart from in front of the historic Wawona Barn, originally built in 1896. After going upstream a short distance along the South Fork Merced River, they return down to the Pioneer Yosemite History Center, a collection of picturesque old buildings from the park's early days.

Following the trail past the tennis courts, they cross the highway and enter Wawona Meadow. After riding through the Wawona Meadow, the group recrosses the highway and travels past the hotel. They then cross the South Fork Merced again, using the covered bridge, and finish up their ride back at the Wawona Barn.

The half-day and all-day rides at Wawona Stables are available by prior arrangement only. For the half-day trips, riders have a choice. They can either go up to Chilnualna Fall or over to Alder Creek Fall. Most riders select the Chilnualna Fall trip. Leaving from the stables at either 8:00 a.m. or 1:00 p.m., they make a rather steep ascent along a trail that at times is shaded by ponderosa pine and incense-cedar.

As they approach the fall, riders have an excellent view of its entire length as it comes roaring down. They continue up to the top, where everyone gets off for a 15-minute break. Looking out from the top of Chilnualna Fall, they have a sweeping view of the Wawona Valley down below. After remounting, they begin the ride back down through the switchbacks to the stables.

On the Alder Fall trip, riders head off on the Alder Creek Trail. They don't make it all the way to Alder Creek Falls, but get close enough to get a good view of the 100-foot high fall. After a break, they return.

The all-day trip, departing at 8:00 a.m., expands on the two half-day trips. Riders leave the stables along the Chilnualna Fall Trail and make the ascent up to the top of the fall. But then instead of turning around, they continue on to Deer Camp, where the group stops for lunch.

After a half-hour to 45-minute break, riders travel down to the Alder Creek Fall and complete the trip along the Alder Creek Trail. For the vacationer wishing to get to know the Wawona area better, the all-day trip clearly offers the most complete experience.

Pack Trips

Wawona Stables also offers spot and extended trips. Among the suggested destinations for spot trips are Johnson Lake, Buena Vista Lake, and Chilnualna Lake. A suggested six-day, five-night extended trip makes stops at Johnson Lake, Moraine Meadow, Triple Fork of the Merced River, Ottoway Lake, and Buena Vista Lake.

Rates

The two-hour ride is $28 and the half-day ride is $38. The all-day ride is $58. For spot and extended trips, a packer is $110 per day. Pack and saddle animals are $59 per day.

Payment Method

Wawona Stables accepts cash, personal checks, traveler's checks, MasterCard, Visa, Diners Club, Discover, and American Express.

Rider Age Limit

Riders must be at least seven years old. Children 12 and under must wear helmets. Helmets are also available for all other riders.

How To Get There

From Highway 99, take Highway 41 east from Fresno. Continue on past Oakhurst to Yosemite National Park. From the entrance, proceed to Wawona. Look for the stables near the Yosemite Pioneer History Center.

YOSEMITE TRAILS PACK STATION

P.O. Box 100
Fish Camp, CA 93623
(209) 683-7611
Owner: Larry Knapp

At over 2,700 years old, the Grizzly Giant certainly ranks as one of planet earth's true senior citizens and it's not alone. In all, there are over

500 mature sequoias in the Mariposa Grove, including some of the oldest redwoods found anywhere.

For that reason alone, the Mariposa Grove is well worth seeing. Yosemite Trails Pack Station, located in Fish Camp just outside the southern border of Yosemite National Park, offers a half-day ride that goes to the edge of the Mariposa Grove. One other ride is also offered by the pack station, which operates from May 15 to October 15 each year, but it's the Mariposa Grove trip that stands out.

Beginning at the pack station, once the site of an old logging camp, riders head off towards the park through a forest of sugar pine, ponderosa pine, and cedar. The trip to the grove takes about two hours and follows Ranier Creek part of the way.

Upon their arrival, riders tie up their horses at the edge of the grove and tour the giant trees on foot. Among the highlights along the clearly-marked path is the Fallen Monarch, a tree that fell possibly centuries ago and, of course, the Grizzly Giant.

Other noteworthy trees are the California Tree, one of two that had tunnels cut through them back in the late 1800s, and the Clothespin Tree, burned by fire to resemble a clothespin. After strolling through the grove and stopping for a picnic lunch, riders remount and travel back along a different trail to the pack station.

For vacationers with less riding experience, Yosemite Trails Pack Station also offers a one-hour ride. From the pack station, riders follow a trail through the heavy forest into a nearby canyon. They continue on a ridge above Big Creek before crossing over and returning back along the other side of the same creek at a lower level. It's a pleasant mountain ride amidst the ferns and the big pines.

Yosemite Trails Pack Station offers a dinner version of this ride as well at 4:00 p.m. each day. After spending an hour on the trail, riders sit down to a meal of steak, corn-on-the-cob, beans, bread, and salad. This is followed by a camp fire program complete with the group singing songs, accompanied by a guitar player, and roasting marshmallows over the crackling fire.

As a convenience for those members of the family who would prefer not to ride, a wagon will pick them up at the nearby Marriott Hotel and transport them to dinner. This allows members of the family of all ages to enjoy the camp fire fun.

Rates

The one-hour ride is $15 per person for four or more riders and $18 per person for groups of less than four. The half-day ride is $40. The dinner ride is $30 and $22 for those who travel by wagon.

Methods Of Payment

Yosemite Trails Pack Station accepts cash, personal checks, traveler's checks, Visa, and MasterCard.

Rider Age Limit

All riders must be at least seven years old.

How To Get There

From Fresno, take Highway 41 towards Yosemite. Just south of Fish Camp, turn right on Jackson Road. Continue for 1-1/4 miles to the pack station.

Father and daughter on the trail above Huntington Lake

D & F PACK STATION

P.O. Box 156
Lakeshore, CA 93634
(415) 946-1475 (W)
(209) 839-3220 (S)
Owner: Brad Meyers

Huntington Lake, located as it is on the edge of the Kaiser Wilderness, is a prime destination for people interested in all forms of outdoor recreation. The area around the lake offers ample opportunities for fishing, hiking, and camping. But best of all for trail riders, it's a great place to ride a horse.

D & F Pack Station, which operates out of its stables in Lakeshore from mid-June to October 1, provides a number of options for interested trail riders. Those interested in spending only a short time in the saddle might consider one of the two-hour rides, scheduled at 9:00 a.m., 11:30 a.m., and 2:30 p.m. each day. One route goes up into the hills above the pack station, while the other takes riders down by the lake.

On the first of the two-hour routes, riders head out along a trail that winds through the forest. They pick up Potter Creek and follow it for some distance, passing through meadows along the way. During the trip, which eventually loops back to the pack station, riders are able to catch glimpses of Huntington Lake through the trees.

The alternative route takes riders right down to the lake. Leaving the pack station, riders travel down past the camp grounds, crossing Deer Creek along the way. From the camp grounds, they swing down by the lake and follow the shoreline all the way down to Cedar Crest Cove. They turn around at Cedar Crest Cove and return along the the same trail, enjoying the spectacle of the many sailboats on the lake as they go.

More experienced riders might consider the half-day ride offered either at 8:00 a.m. or 1:00 p.m. It begins along the same route as the first two-hour trip. But it then follows Potter Creek right up towards the Kaiser Wilderness. Crossing Potter Pass, at 9,100 feet in elevation, riders catch a view of the craggy Minarets off in the distance and the back side of Mammoth Mountain Ski Area.

Continuing over the pass, they enter the Kaiser Wilderness and then continue on to Twin Lakes. At the lakes, they get off their horses for a 10-minute leg stretch. Then they head back down, completing the trip along the second half of the two-hour ride trail.

Without question, however, the most scenic views are on the all-day trip, departing each day at 8:00 a.m. Following the Kaiser Loop Trail, riders enter the Kaiser Wilderness almost immediately, and begin a 3,000 foot climb up to Kaiser Peak. Along the way, they pass 9,076 foot high College Rock and cross Bear Creek, before reaching Kaiser Peak at 10,320 feet in elevation. From the top of the peak, which has snow on its shady side all year round, the 360° view is simply breathtaking.

After enjoying lunch, riders continue along the Kaiser Loop Trail, passing Nellie Lake, traveling through Marys Meadow and crossing Line Creek, before returning to the stables. Overall, riders on the all-day trip can expect to spend about six hours in the saddle.

An alternative version of the all-day trip to Kaiser Peak can also be arranged, especially for fishermen. Instead of concentrating on catching great views, riders on this trip can concentrate on catching that big one.

Pack Trips

With four wilderness areas nearby to serve – Kaiser Wilderness, Dinkey Lakes Wilderness, Ansel Adams Wilderness, and John Muir Wilderness – D & F Pack Station does a tremendous amount of spot packing. However, they do offer all-inclusive trips, as well, for groups of four or more people. The most popular is a base camp trip from Lake Edison to Grassy Meadow, near Grassy Lake. During their stay, riders take day trips to Wilbur May Lake, Olive Lake, and the other excellent fishing spots

Rates

The two-hour ride is $20 and the half-day ride is $35. All-day trips are $60. All-inclusive pack trips are $135 per person per day. For spot and extended trips, saddle and pack animals are $40 per day, the packer is $60 per day, and the packer's horse is $40 per day.

Payment Method

D & F Pack Station accepts cash, personal checks, traveler's checks, MasterCard, and VISA.

Rider Age Limit

On the shorter rides, children five and under may double. For longer trips, children must be at least six years old.

How To Get There

From Clovis, proceed to Lakeshore at Huntington Lake. Go past the general store and restaurant, and look for the pack station sign on the right. Turn off the main road and follow the dirt road up to the pack station.

HIGH SIERRA PACK STATION

Mono Hot Springs, CA 93613
(Winter Address)
P.O. Box 1166
Clovis, CA 93613
(209) 299-8297
Owner: John and Jenise Cunningham

The road to Florence and Edison Lakes, deep in the backcountry of the western Sierra, is not for the faint of heart. Its excruciating twists and heart-stopping turns will leave even the most experienced drivers begging for the relief of a straight-away. But for those who can successfully negotiate this intimidating ribbon of blacktop, there are visual delights awaiting that are unmatched anywhere else in California outside of the national parks.

Best of all, when the road ends, there's a way to keep going even further into the scenic Sierra wilderness. High Sierra Pack Station, operating out of both Florence Lake and Edison Lake from June 15 to October 15, offers trail rides that travel through countryside rarely seen by anyone but determined backpackers.

There's also an extra bonus for those taking trips out of Florence Lake. They are personally guided by the legendary Mono Bob, a retired school teacher who delights in sharing his knowledge of the history, geology, flora, and fauna of the Florence Lake area.

On his two-hour trips, for instance, riders head down behind the Florence Lake Dam, completed in 1926 by the Southern California Edison Company. At its base, Mono Bob tells the whole history of the Big Creek-San Joaquin hydroelectric project that was developed in the region during the early part of this century.

From the dam, the riders' trail drops down into Jackass Meadow, actually a series of meadows, that's bordered by a stand of aspen. As the group travels through these beautiful meadows, Mono Bob points out holes in the ground once used for grinding corn by the Mono Indians, the original inhabitants of the area. Farther along the trail, he takes riders through what once served as an arrowhead factory. If riders look closely, they can sometimes even spot pieces of obsidian left over from those ancient times.

After crossing over the South Fork San Joaquin River, the group swings around and returns to the pack station. For riders with only limited time, Mono Bob also does a one-hour version of this same trip. In addition, when the meadows are too soggy, he leads an alternative two-hour trip that goes down along the south side of Florence Lake and back.

Mono Bob on the shores of Florence Lake

The half-day ride follows the same route as the alternative two-hour trip, but instead of turning around, riders continue on to a bridge that crosses the San Joaquin River near the upper end of Florence Lake. Looking off from the bridge, riders catch an outstanding view of 10,862 foot high Ward Mountain and 11,020 foot high Mount Shinn.

Nearby, Mono Bob shows off the highlight of the half-day trip, a 50-foot high waterfall that cascades down to form a natural ladder for brown trout heading upstream to their spawning grounds. After a break for lunch, the group mounts up and returns back down along the lake.

For the most spectacular views, however, the trip to consider is the all-day ride. Leaving at 8:00 a.m., riders begin a tough climb up a rugged, rocky trail that gains 2,000 feet in elevation in the first three miles. They pass through Manse Meadow, resplendently bedecked with wildflowers during the middle of the summer, before reaching Dutch Lake. They then swing along a second trail for another mile or so to a beautiful mountain lake sitting in a natural crater named appropriately Crater Lake.

Normally, riders stay at the lake for about four hours allowing ample time to fish, to take pictures, or to chat with Mono Bob. As they leave the lake on the trip back down, riders have a magnificent panoramic view of the whole Sierra crest. Shifting their gaze to the southeast, they can look across five ridges all the way into the Evolution Valley. In the distance, they can even spot Mount Darwin.

Continuing down the trail, riders pass juniper trees that are more than 2,500 years old, rivaling even the venerable sequoias for perseverance and longevity. Eventually, after a steep descent they reach the pack station.

At nearby Thomas A. Edison Lake, the rides are also quite scenic, though they come without Mono Bob's engaging commentary. On the shortest of these, the one-hour trip, riders take off through a forest of ponderosa pine, Jeffrey pine, and red fir, before entering a nearby meadow. They continue across a meandering creek and into a second meadow. The trail then takes them up around a volcanic ridge that offers a display of volcanic rock mixed in with granite. From there, they loop back down to the pack station.

The two-hour ride is a loop up to a slightly misnamed Twin Meadows. There are, in fact, four meadows strung out in a series. The first is quite lush and green, but the other three are each progressively drier. As they swing back around to return from Twin Meadows along a different trail, riders can look down on Lake Edison tucked in the forest below.

There are two choices for the half-day trip. Riders can either go up to Devil's Bathtub, a small lake in the John Muir Wilderness or over to Graveyard Meadows, which sits just inside the wilderness boundary. On the Devil's Bathtub trip, they head out along the same trail taken for the two-hour ride to Twin Meadows, continuing on through the forest, gaining elevation as they go.

At the lake, they have an excellent view of 11, 494 foot Graveyard Peak and they can see Lake Edison several miles below. After a half-hour stop, they head back down the trail.

On the trip to Graveyard Meadows, riders take a fork off the Devil's Bathtub trail that heads northeast. After traveling through the forest, they arrive at Graveyard Meadows, two huge expanses of green grass and multi-colored wildflowers separated by trees. They stop at the first meadow for about 30 minutes, before heading back. On the return trip, riders catch a view of Lake Edison and, off in the distance, Bear Ridge.

The all-day trip also goes to Devil's Bathtub, but instead of a 30-minute stop, riders have several hours to fish. As an alternative, they can go to Arrowhead Lake up above Graveyard Meadows.

Pack Trips

Though they are not prescheduled, High Sierra Pack Station does offer interesting all-inclusive trips. Most popular are the base camps trips, which typically go to either Rosemarie Meadow or Lou Beverly Lake. From these spots located near the John Muir Trail, riders take day trips to nearby lakes and streams that offer excellent golden trout fishing.

Rates

The one-hour ride is $10 and the two-hour ride is $20. The half-day ride is $35 and the all-day ride is $50. All-inclusive pack trips are $125 per person per day and there is a four-person, four-day minimum. Spot and extended trips are $90 per day for a packer with horse and $45 per day for riding or pack animals. Reservations are required for all trips, including the day rides.

Method of Payment

High Sierra Pack Station accepts cash, personal checks, traveler's checks, and money orders.

Rider Age Limit

There is no set age limit for riders. However, children five and under must double with a parent.

How To Get There

From Clovis, take Highway 168 and proceed to Huntington Lake. From Huntington Lake, take the Kaiser Pass Road. At a fork in the road two miles from Mono Hot Springs, either go right to Florence Lake or left to Lake Edison. Each road is approximately seven miles long. Follow the signs to the pack stations at each lake.

MUIR TRAIL RANCH

P.O. Box 176
Lakeshore, CA 93634
(Winter Address)
P.O. Box 269
Ahwahnee, CA 93601
(209) 966-3195
Owner: Adeline Smith

There are thousands of trails in the Sierra Nevada. Some are short little paths. Others cross vast stretches of territory. But none are more dramatic or offer more unforgettable scenery than the legendary John Muir Trail. Extending 212 miles from Mount Whitney to Yosemite Valley, this special tribute to America's greatest conservationist passes through three national parks, one national monument, and four national wilderness areas.

Remarkably, it also passes right by one of the most unique, and certainly one of the most inaccessible, guest ranches in all of America, the Muir Trail Ranch. As the only private property along this historic trail, the 200 acres of the Muir Trail Ranch offers vacationers an experience the likes of which they simply can't find anywhere else.

Getting there, however, is a major undertaking, but then that only adds to its charm. To reach the ranch, vacationers must first conquer the winding, single-lane road up to Florence Lake, certainly one of the more intimidating stretches of blacktop in the Sierra Nevada. But that's just the beginning. At Florence Lake, they take a passenger ferry boat to the southeast end of the lake and then they ride by horseback to the ranch. The final leg of the journey up the San Joaquin River Canyon takes between one-and-a-half and two hours.

The Muir Trail Ranch, located at 7,700 feet in elevation, was originally started as a cattle ranch back in 1897. In the 1930s, the property, then called the Diamond D, was developed into a guest ranch and has continued as such to the present day. Unlike in earlier times, however, it now caters only to groups, ranging from 15 to 20 persons. Individuals and couples can sometimes arrange to fill out a group, but for the most part, the ranch is best suited for groups formed out of three or four families pooling their resources. Reservations can be made for these groups from June to October each year.

The principal activity at the Muir Trail Ranch, of course, is horseback riding, as the journey into the ranch on the traditional arrival day of Saturday indicates. Sundays, however, are rest days for the horses, so guests don't get a chance to climb back into the saddle until Monday morning. But from then on, for the balance of the week, guests can go on daily rides and overnight trips to destinations of their choosing.

Among the places most frequently visited on day rides are Sallie Keyes Lakes, Piute Creek, Lou Beverly Lake, and the bridge over the Middle Fork San Joaquin near Florence Lake. The northwest corner of Kings Canyon National Park is also within easy riding distance.

Overnight trips are often planned into the Evolution Valley or the Goddard Canyon area. Sallie Keyes Lakes and Rose Lake are also popular overnight destinations.

Other Activities

For those who prefer to rely on their own two legs for transportation rather than on the four-legged kind, the opportunities are limited only by their stamina and imagination. High Sierra scenery of all descriptions is within reasonable hiking distance of the ranch. Even Kings Canyon National Park is only three miles away.

The fishing in the region, of course, is outstanding. Within a short distance of the ranch, guests can reach pristine alpine lakes, gentle mountain streams, and raging backcountry rivers that are home to brown, eastern brook, rainbow, and golden trout. Only fly fishing on a catch and release basis is permitted on ranch property, but away from the ranch guests may use lures, bait, or whatever strikes their fancy.

The remote mountain location is also ideal for photography, birdwatching, and nature study. In addition, the ranch offers what just may be the ultimate in relaxation – two wonderful natural hot spring baths, one 107°F and the other 98°F. With privacy provided by rough-hewn log walls, guests can slide thigh deep into the mineral-rich, odor-free baths built out of stone and soak languidly in serene splendor. They can gaze up at the clear, blue sky above, glance over at the neatly-tended beds of wildflowers nearby, or just close their eyes and float a thousand miles away. For the person fleeing the stresses of nine-to-five slavery, it doesn't get much better than this.

Accommodations

As one might expect in a location so remote, the accommodations are fairly rustic. But, surprisingly, the ranch does have electricity, thanks to its 1920s-vintage hydroelectric power plant. So heat and light are available throughout.

Guests may stay in one of eight log cabins located along the bank of a stream, or they can bed down in one of the wooden-floored tent cabins down near the San Joaquin River. The log cabins all have bathrooms that include a cold-water sink and toilet. Guests staying in the tent cabins, however, are obliged to use a central bathroom facility. Hot-water bathing, of course, can be done at the hot springs.

Where individuals choose to stay, however, must be decided by the members of the group themselves. Individual cabins are not rented, the entire ranch is made available for one flat fee. The minimum weekly rent for the Muir Trail Ranch is $5,250 for the first 15 people, plus the leader who goes free. Each additional person over 16 is another $350. Children under five may come free and do not count towards the 20-person ranch maximum.

In theory, a couple could rent the entire ranch for themselves, although that becomes rather an expensive proposition. Probably a better approach is for couples or individuals to indicate an interest in staying at the ranch, and if a group has extra room, they may be included.

Dining

Those expecting Club Med-style dining would probably be happier somewhere else. All food and food preparation is the responsibility of the group renting the ranch. Fortunately, this can be handled in more than one way. The members of the group can take care of it themselves, of course, or they can hire a cook. They can also hire a caterer to take care of everything, including the ranch cleanup. A catering organization is available to do just that.

However a group decides to handle the cooking, there are excellent facilities available at the ranch. The fully-equiped kitchen has two restaurant-style stoves, a Cuisinart food processor, a commercial food slicer, a three-carafe coffee maker, and a commercial dishwasher. In addition, the kitchen has a 500 cubic foot walk-in freezer and a continuous supply of ice cubes is produced by two automatic machines. Of course, all necessary utensils are available.

Meals can be enjoyed either in an indoor dining room or out on a terrace that's equipped with a wood-burning barbecue.

The Muir Trail Ranch probably isn't for everyone. But for those who can appreciate its unique charms, it can offer the ultimate in guest ranch experiences.

Horse Rental Rates

Horses may be rented for the Saturday rides into or out from the ranch for $25, which includes the guide. During their stay at the ranch, guests may rent a horse for $35 per day. There is an additional charge of $75 per day for a guide, who can accompany up to 10 riders.

Method Of Payment

The Muir Trail Ranch accepts cash and personal checks.

Rider Age Limit

Children must be at least six years old to ride a horse.

Nearest Airport

The closest commercial airport is located in Fresno.

How To Get There

From Clovis, take Highway 168 and proceed to Huntington Lake. From Huntington Lake, take the Kaiser Pass Road. At a fork in the road two miles from Mono Hot Springs, go right to Florence Lake. Continue seven miles to Florence Lake. Look for the signs for the Florence Resort. Take the ferry across the lake. Then either walk or ride a horse up the canyon to the ranch.

The stables at Pebble Beach Equestrian Center

CENTRAL COAST 8

PEBBLE BEACH EQUESTRIAN CENTER

P.O. Box 1519
Pebble Beach, CA 93953
(408) 624-2756
Owner: Pebble Beach Company

Bing Crosby's televised Pro-Am Clambake introduced this private residential and resort community to millions all over the world. Its haunting cypress trees, verdant pine forests, and craggy coastline have inspired artists and writers for years.

There are still some untouched areas in Pebble Beach left to explore. There is also a perfect way to explore them. Twice each day, except Mondays, at 10:00 a.m. and 2:00 p.m., the Pebble Beach Equestrian Center offers one-hour trail rides. What makes these rides particularly unusual is that the Pebble Beach Equestrian Center is the one place in California that offers trail rides using English saddles exclusively.

In all other ways, however, it's your typical trail ride. From the stables, which served as the setting for parts of the movie *National Velvet* with Elizabeth Taylor, riders head into a thick forest of Monterey pines. These tall, straight, fast-growing trees at one time grew only in this area and nowhere else.

Along the trail, it's not uncommon to spot a young doe dashing into the brush. At times, the trail emerges from the woods and takes riders past stately Pebble Beach homes. At other points in the trip, it goes by some of the fairways on the renowned Spyglass Hill Golf Course.

Eventually, the forest opens out onto sand dunes, and riders get a great view of the spectacular rocky shoreline not far away. Then it's back through the woods and home to the stables.

One thing to keep in mind, if you decide to go riding in Pebble Beach, is that you need advance reservations. The Pebble Beach Equestrian Center limits each ride to four horses, so individual trips can fill up quickly. If you have a reservation, you can enter Pebble Beach without paying the tollgate charge.

Be sure to bring along a sweater or jacket in case the fog rolls in. It's beautiful to look at as it creeps through the trees, but it can chill you to the bone.

Rates

The charge for the one-hour ride is $30.

Payment Method

The Pebble Beach Equestrian Center accepts cash, personal checks, and traveler's checks.

Rider Age Limit

Riders must be at least 12 years old.

How To Get There

From Highway 1, take the Pebble Beach exit. Enter Pebble Beach at the tollgate and proceed along 17 Mile Drive. Continue past the Pebble Beach Golf Links and The Lodge at Pebble Beach. When you reach Portola Road, turn left. The Pebble Beach Equestrian Center will be on your right.

VENTANA WILDERNESS EXPEDITIONS

Tassajara Road
Star Route, Box 94
Carmel Valley, CA 93924
(408) 659-0433
Owner: Fred Nason, Sr.

Only a few miles inland from California's spectacular Big Sur Coast, and extending all the way across to Carmel Valley, is an area as primitive and untamed as any in the state. Known as the Ventana Wilderness, it's a particularly rugged portion of the mountainous Los Padres National Forest, where mountain lions and bobcats still roam.

Normally, it's accessible only on foot. But, for people who love horses, Ventana Wilderness Expeditions, located near the Tassajara Zen Center in upper Carmel Valley, offers two-, three-, four-, and five-day all-inclusive trail rides that go into the heart of the Ventana Wilderness.

For people who don't have the time for a long trip, but still want to get a taste of the Ventana Wilderness, the two-day ride should more than fill the bill. Starting at the Los Padres Dam in Carmel Valley, riders take a trail that follows the Carmel River as it snakes its way upstream through canyons overgrown with trees and brush. Because the trail follows the river so closely, there are countless stream crossings for the riders to make.

The group stops for the night at either Carmel River Camp, Hiding Camp, or Buckskin Flat Camp, depending upon the availability of camp sites. The following day, the group returns down the same trail.

The three-day ride covers less territory than the two-day trip, but it offers an opportunity for greater relaxation. From Chews Ridge, riders travel five miles down a trail to Pine Valley, an idyllic spot sheltered by tall Ponderosa pines and close to a large, open meadow.

During their stay, riders may take short hikes, examine the interesting rock formations near camp, or visit the waterfall and natural pool a short distance downstream. On the third day, the group heads back up the five-mile trail to Chews Ridge.

Maybe the most unusual trail ride offered by Ventana Wilderness Expeditions is described as "The Spiritual Mountain Expedition." Led by a descendent of the Esselen Indians, riders on this journey learn about the Native American tribe that once made the wilderness near Big Sur their home.

Following the same trail taken on the three-day trip, riders head to Pinc Valley, where a base camp is established. From there, they take day trips. One day, the group rides south past Church Creek Divide to explore caves once used by the Esselens. Another day, they ride to Big Pines. This area was sacred to the Esselens.

Back at the ranch near Chews Ridge, the leader conducts a Sweat Lodge Ceremony in an authentic sweat lodge built behind the barn. In all, it's an introduction to an aspect of Native American culture not to be found anywhere else.

For many people, though, the ultimate Ventana Wilderness trail ride is the five-day trip on the Pine Ridge Trail from Carmel Valley to Pfeiffer Big Sur State Park. The Pine Ridge Trail offers more changes in terrain, vegetation, and scenery than any other in the region. Along the way, riders pass through groves of redwoods and visit the natural hot springs at Cienega Creek.

At Sykes Camp, they can swim in a deep, natural pool in the Big Sur River. Eventually, the trail emerges from the wilderness and drops down into Pfeiffer Big Sur State Park, where the riders end their journey under the shade of the towering redwoods.

Rates

The standard charge is $125 per day for these all-inclusive trips.

Payment Method

Ventana Wilderness Expeditions accepts cash, personal checks, and traveler's checks.

Rider Age Limit

All riders must be at least seven years old.

How To Get There

From Highway 1 near Carmel, turn onto Carmel Valley Road. Go past Carmel Valley Village well into upper Carmel Valley. At the Tassajara Road, turn right. From Highway 101 near Greenfield, take the Arroyo Seco exit. Head west on Carmel Valley Road. At Tassajara Road, turn left. Then continue on the road even after the pavement ends. Just before you reach the ranger station on Chew Ridge, you will come to the ranch on the right.

MOLERA TRAIL RIDES

Andrew Molera State Park
Highway 1
Big Sur, CA 93920
(408) 625-8664
Owner: Fred Nason, Sr.

Some 35 years ago, celebrated author Henry Miller wrote of his beloved Big Sur, "This is the face of the land as the Creator intended it to look." In the years that have followed, little about this isolated refuge from the ravages of civilization has changed. From its towering redwoods to its pounding surf, Big Sur remains a place of uncommon beauty.

The beach at Andrew Molera State Park

The good news for trail riders is that the unique Big Sur experience can be enjoyed on horseback. From April to November, Molera Trail Rides, located on the edge of the 2,088 acre Andrew Molera State Park, offers scenic two-hour trail rides. The rides begin at 10:00 a.m., 12:00 noon, and 3:00 p.m. During the summer months, there is an additional ride in the evening that is timed to put riders in perfect position to watch the sun set over the ocean. It departs at 6:00 p.m.

As the two-hour trip begins, riders cross the Big Sur River, pass through a forest of redwoods, and head out into an open meadow. Looking east, they can see the rugged Santa Lucia Mountains.

During the springtime, poppies and lupines dot the meadow. Overhead, riders can often spot a red-tail hawk slowly riding a thermal.

Eventually, the trail heads out to the beach. As riders move along the high tide line, waves slap up near the hooves of the horses. Off to the north, they can see the rocky promontory of the Point Sur Lighthouse. Looking south, they can follow the coastline with their eyes down to a point just north of Pfeiffer Beach.

From the beach, riders head up to a bluff that offers a panoramic view of the whole coastal region. On the evening ride, this wind-swept bluff is where they stop to watch the sunset. The trip then returns through the meadow, across the river, and back to the stables.

Two suggestions for those going on a trail ride in Andrew Molera State Park: Bring along a windbreaker, because out by the water there is a constant strong wind. Also, be on the lookout for poison oak. There are places along the trail where you are surrounded by it and the horses are absolutely oblivious.

Rates

The basic two-hour ride is $50. Private two-hour rides are $75. A special three-hour Honeymoon Ride, which includes lunch, is $90.

Payment Method

Molera Trail Rides accepts cash, personal checks, and traveler's checks.

Rider Age Limit

Riders must be at least seven years old.

How To Get There

From Carmel, head south on Highway 1 and continue for 22 miles. Turn right at the sign for Andrew Molera State Park. Don't enter the park. Continue down the dirt road and you will reach the stables at the end.

LIVERY STABLE

1207 Silver Spur Place
Oceano, CA 93433
(805) 489-8100
Owner: Livery Stable, Inc.

Horseback riding is nothing new to the area around Pismo Beach. Back in 1849, when Jose Ortega first established Rancho el Pismo in what is today Pismo Beach, horses, along with cattle, were what he principally raised.

In more recent times, this pleasant coastal community has become better known for its famous clams and its 23 miles of white sandy beaches. But the tradition of horseback riding lives on.

Livery Stables, located just south of Pismo Beach in Oceano, rents horses for up to two hours of unescorted riding on the beach. For those who would prefer a guide, local teenagers are available to assist them in return for a tip.

The huge dunes to the west of the stables are the only areas off limits to riders. The rest of the beach from the dunes to the Pismo Beach Pier is available for wide-open riding. For anyone who has ever dreamed of racing along the tideline on a horse, this is the place on the Central Coast.

The entire trip to the Pismo Beach Pier and back takes approximately two hours. Along the way, riders can enjoy all the sights and sounds the sea has to offer, including the dolphins that frolic close to shore.

Before you consider this particular excursion, however, be sure to check the wind conditions. A strong wind can really kick up the sand and make the whole riding experience unpleasant for both you and your horse.

Livery Stable is open 8:00 a.m. to 5:00 p.m. daily during the summer and 8:00 a.m. to 4:00 p.m. Wednesday through Monday during the winter.

Rates

The standard charge is $15 an hour. The maximum rental is two hours. A $25 deposit is required, when a horse is taken out.

Payment Method

Livery Stable accepts only cash.

Rider Age Limit

Riders must be at least eight years old to ride alone. Children two through seven may double with a parent at no extra charge.

How To Get There

From Highway 101, take the Highway 1 turnoff. Follow Highway 1 until you reach 22nd Street in Oceano. From the south turn left on 22nd Street. From the north turn right. Take 22nd Street until you reach Silver Spur Place. Follow Silver Spur Place to the end.

THE ALISAL GUEST RANCH

1054 Alisal Road
Solvang, CA 93963
(805) 688-6411
Owners: The Jackson Family

Just down the road from the Danish community of Solvang and a mere 40 miles north of Santa Barbara sits one of the most popular and well-respected guest ranches in all of California – The Alisal Ranch.

Spread over 10,000 acres of pasture land and rolling hills, The Alisal has been a working cattle ranch since the 18th century. As a guest ranch, it offers a wonderful array of activities, comfortable accommodations, and a tradition of hospitality that brings families back year after year.

For anyone who loves horseback riding or would like to learn, The Alisal is paradise. There are dozens of different riding trails on the sprawling ranch that offer an interesting variety of scenery and terrain. Expert wranglers lead the trips, which are divided into three groups according to ability – beginning, intermediate, and advanced.

The beginners generally stick to the flatter terrain and never go beyond a walk. Intermediate riders travel over more varied terrain and do some trotting. Advanced riders get to tackle the toughest trails and have several opportunities to go at a full gallop.

The rides, always two hours in length, start at 10:00 a.m. and 2:00 p.m. everyday. With so many trails to choose from, the wranglers usually find a different way to go each time they take a group out.

Looking back down from the ridges above the ranch, riders catch a panoramic view of Solvang, and a large section of the Santa Ynez Valley, stretched out before them. On some trips, they can even spot the homes of celebrities who live in the area, such as Bo Derek and Jimmy Connors.

Probably the most interesting sights along the trails at The Alisal are the many birds and animals that make this area their home. The Alisal is a game preserve, so there is a remarkable abundance of wildlife.

Along the trail, riders may spot coyotes, mountain lions, bobcats, badgers, wild pigs, and even the occasional bear. There are also countless deer in the area, and eagles sometimes soar overhead. It all makes for a delightful time in the saddle and a wonderful stay at the ranch.

Other Activities

There is plenty to do when you're not out on the trail. Golfers can get in some swings on the 18-hole, par 72 golf course. A PGA professional is in residence throughout the year, and cart and club rentals are always available. Green fees are $45.

Tennis players can play on one of the seven tennis courts. Lessons are available from a certified pro. Court rental is $10 per hour.

Down at Lake Alisal, guests can rent rowboats, sailboats, and windsurfing equipment. Or they can try their luck with a fishing pole.

Swimmers and sunbathers will enjoy the large, heated pool and the hot water spa nearby. Joggers will appreciate the special half-mile jogging course. Near the swimming pool, guests will find horseshoe, croquet, shuffleboard, badminton, and volleyball equipment. Next door to the recreation room, guests can play ping pong or pool.

Accommodations

Guests stay in sixty attractive, comfortable units. A large studio room with twin beds and a wood-burning fireplace is $255 per day, double occupancy. A large studio room with a king-size bed, an outside patio, and a wood-burning fireplace can range from $275 to $330 per day, double occupancy. A large bedroom with king or twin beds, and a sitting room with studio beds and a wood-burning fireplace can range from $295 to $330 per day, double occupancy. There is a charge of $65 for each additional person (two years and up). The minimum stay is two nights. Breakfast and dinner are included in the basic room rate.

Dining

Over the years, The Alisal has earned a well-deserved reputation for exceptional dining. Dinner, best described as California Continental with a gourmet flair, typically features from four to five different entrees each evening. During the meal, gentlemen are required to wear jackets.

Such formality is not necessary at breakfast. Guests either select from the many delights on the buffet table or order their favorites from the menu. Lunch, of course, is not included in the room rate, but guests may purchase sandwiches and burgers at the snack bar. During the cool winter months, lunch is available in the dining room.

Horse Rental Rates

The two-hour trail rides, which are available for guests of The Alisal only, cost $40. Special package rates are also available that include unlimited horseback riding.

Payment Method

The Alisal accepts cash, personal checks, traveler's checks, Visa, MasterCard, and American Express.

Rider Age Limit

All riders must be at least seven years old. Younger children may be walked on a horse with a lead rope.

Nearest Airport

The closest commercial airport is located in Santa Barbara. Private pilots, however, may land at Santa Ynez Airport

How To Get There

From Highway 101 near Buelton, take the Solvang/Lompoc exit. Turn onto Highway 246 and head for Solvang. Turn right on Alisal Road. Proceed to the main gate of The Alisal Ranch.

CIRCLE BAR B GUEST RANCH

1800 Refugio Road
Goleta, CA 93117
(805) 968-1113
Owners: The Brown Family

There are no signs that there is anything unusual about Refugio Road, the two-lane blacktop that winds up through a scenic canyon in the Santa Ynez Mountains. Except for the occasional appearance of a black limousine, accompanied by two Suburbans containing Secret Servicemen, it looks like just another country road. But a few years ago, it was the only route to one of the most important addresses in America–the Western White House.

The image of former President Ronald Reagan riding a horse around the ranch is still fresh in the minds of many Americans. What few may realize is that they can ride around in the hills right near the Reagan Ranch themselves. The Circle Bar B Guest Ranch, located five miles down the road, offers several trail rides, including one that goes up on the ridge just south of the Reagan Ranch.

Besides giving you a taste of Reagan country, the rides offer some of the best views of the California coast you will find anywhere. In addition, the Circle Bar B is one of only a handful of places where riders can gallop.

The Circle Bar B offers its most popular ride, one and half hours in length, at 9:30, 11:30, 2:00, and 4:00 every day. On weekdays, a 6:30 p.m. ride is added. From the stables, riders head up a trail that is shaded by sycamores and alder. A small creek runs along nearby. The riders gain elevation as they turn on to a dirt road. It is here, on the dirt road, that the horses trot, lope, and then break into a full gallop. They come to a stop at a point in the road that offers outstanding views of the coast below.

The Santa Ynez Mountains near the Reagan Ranch

The group then turns around and heads back down the hill. Along the way, they can catch a glimpse of a small waterfall. The trail then heads through an avocado orchard and back down to the stables.

The premier ride at the Circle Bar B Guest Ranch, however, is the half-day ride. Once a day at 9:00 a.m., a wrangler leads riders up through the wooded canyon into the chaparral that covers the upper portions of the Santa Ynez Mountains. The chaparral, a tangled mixture of manzanita, scrub oak, toyon, yucca, and holly-leaf cherry, surrounds the riders as they reach the crest of the ridge just south of the Reagan Ranch.

As the path continues along the ridge, the view is spectacular. On one side, riders can look down on the town of Solvang in the Santa Ynez Valley. On the other side, they have a panoramic view of the entire coast from Gaviota Beach to the University of California at Santa Barbara.

During the trip, the riders stop for a picnic lunch. Following lunch, they return back down through the chaparral and head to the stables.

On weekdays, the Circle Bar B Guest Ranch also offers a two-and-a-half hour ride at 9:00 a.m. and 2:00 p.m. It offers better views than the one-and-a-half hour ride, but less time in the saddle than the half-day ride.

Horse Rental Rates

There is a two-tiered rate system. The one-and-a-half-hour ride is $23 for overnight guests and $25 for non-guests. The two-and-a-half-hour ride is $40 for both guests and non-guests. The half-day ride is $50 for guests and $57 for non-guests. In addition, the management has placed a sign in the stable's area that encourages riders to tip the wranglers.

Payment Method

The Circle Bar B Guest Ranch accepts cash, personal checks, traveler's checks, Visa, and MasterCard.

Rider Age Limit

Riders must be at least seven years old or have proven riding ability.

Other Activities

For those interested in an overnight stay at a guest ranch, the Circle Bar B offers an experience quite different from that found at The Alisal, located nearby. There are fewer activities available, particularly for children, and there is less of a big ranch feeling. But the setting is quite peaceful, and the ranch offers a refreshing escape for those living a fast-lane life in the city.

The Circle Bar B, which sits just off the road, consists of a collection of red wooden-sided cabins and ranch buildings tucked in among the trees on a gently sloping hill. There is also a pool area and an open-air spa. For entertainment in the evening, guests can stroll down to the dinner theater near the stable area, where they can see a live comedy performance by a local acting group.

Accommodations

The Circle Bar B Guest Ranch offers three types of rooms. The two-bedroom cabin with wet bar and fireplace is $225 a day for two people. An additional child is $60 and an additional adult is $75. The private cabin with fireplace and deck is $186 a day for two people. An additional adult is $75. The private cabin with fireplace and deck is $186 a day for two people. An additional child in a loft is $60 and an additional adult in a loft is $75. A ranch room with a private bath is $128 a day for two people and $85 for a single. An additional child is $50 and an additional adult is $65. The rate includes all meals.

Dining

Guests who work up big appetites on the trail are certain to satisfy them in the Circle Bar B dining room. All meals are served buffet style and guests can go back as many times as they want. On Fridays and Saturdays, tri-tips are featured on the buffet table.

A full hot breakfast is served buffet style and guests can choose either a hot buffet lunch or a picnic lunch.

Nearest Airport

The nearest commercial airport is located in nearby Santa Barbara.

How To Get There

From Highway 101, 20 miles north of Santa Barbara, take the Refugio Road exit. Head east up the road for three and a half miles. Look for the Circle Bar B Guest Ranch on the right.

SAN YSIDRO RANCH

900 San Ysidro Lane
Montecito, CA 93108
(805) 969-5046
Owners: Bob Harmon and Claude Rouas

When Richard Henry Dana first set eyes on the Santa Barbara area back in 1834, one of the things that particularly impressed him was what he described as "an amphitheater of mountains." He was referring, of course, to the Santa Ynez Mountains, which more than anything else give the area its unique identity.

Modern day visitors can enjoy these mountains not only from a distance, but also up close. The San Ysidro Ranch, located in fashionable Montecito, offers trail rides that go up into a section of the Santa Ynez Mountains south of Santa Barbara.

Once co-owned by actor Ronald Coleman, the San Ysidro Ranch has been a favorite resort destination for the rich and famous for years. John F. Kennedy and wife Jacqueline even spent part of their honeymoon there. But despite its exclusive air, the San Ysidro Ranch places no restrictions on its trail rides. They are open to both guests and non-guests.

Everyday at 10:30 a.m. and 2:30 p.m., the San Ysidro Ranch offers a one-hour trail ride for up to five people. There is an added 3:30 p.m. ride on Saturdays and a special 9:00 a.m. ride on Sundays.

Heading out onto a paved road, riders proceed south for about two blocks through a neighborhood of exclusive homes. They then move off onto a dirt trail that winds past the back yards of some of these homes. Clumps of ferns and poison oak poke out onto the trail and rangy old oak trees create a tunnel of shade.

As the riders continue to gain elevation, they leave the residential area and move into the chaparral that is found all along the upper parts of the Santa Ynez Mountains. There are occasional rock outcroppings, and at one point the trail passes a small stream.

The riders proceed north along a ridge that offers views of the coast that are similar to, but somewhat different from those found near the Reagan Ranch. They can see across the city of Santa Barbara to the coast and down past Carpenteria. They also get an excellent view of the Channel Islands out to the west.

As they continue along the ridge, the riders may spot quail near the trail. Rabbits frequently chase by and an occasional a red-tail hawk floats overhead. Eventually, the group will head back down to the stables along a portion of the San Ysidro Trail.

The San Ysidro Ranch also offers a two-hour private ride. It offers experienced riders the opportunity to enjoy even more spectacular views. There is a limit of five people on the private rides.

Rates

The one-hour ride is $35. The two-hour private ride is $100. Advance reservations are required for all rides. Note: The San Ysidro Ranch is a fine hotel with excellent overnight accommodations. However, it is not a guest ranch by definition, so information about accommodations has not been included.

Payment Method

The San Ysidro Ranch accepts cash, personal checks, traveler's checks, Visa, and MasterCard.

Rider Age Limit

Riders must be at least five years old and no doubling is permitted.

How To Get There

From Highway 101, take the San Ysidro Road exit. Head east on San Ysidro Road. Turn right on San Ysidro Lane and go up the driveway into the San Ysidro Ranch. Follow the driveway as it curves left. Then turn right through the maintenance area. The stables are just past the maintenance area on the right.

The corral at Mineral King Pack Station

SOUTHERN SIERRA 9

M BAR J GUEST RANCH

P.O. Box 67
Badger, CA 93603
(209) 337-2513
Owner: Archie & Bunny Stockebrand

Just 18 miles from the entrance to Kings Canyon National Park in the rolling, tree-covered foothills of the Sierras sits the M Bar J Guest Ranch. Operated as a guest ranch since 1946, it's a friendly, down-home place where guests are treated like members of the family.

The informal tone is set almost from the moment guests arrive. After unpacking their bags, everyone climbs on a horse and heads off to a nearby lake for a cookout. At the lake, Archie Stockebrand, the ranch owner and head outdoor chef, barbecues up teriyaki steaks and the guests all get a chance to socialize.

The following morning they begin a regular schedule of trail rides that continues throughout the week. Every day, except Tuesday, guests go riding for about two-and-a-half hours. Half the group goes in the morning from 9:30 a.m. to noon. The other half goes out in the afternoon from 2:00 p.m. to 4:30 p.m. The order of the groups switches each day.

Typically, a ride will go up and down through the surrounding foothills, which are covered with live oak, buckeye, and manzanita. Along the way, riders encounter numerous ground squirrels and quail scurrying around. Deer and coyotes also make an appearance from time to time. On one of the trips, riders climb from the ranch, sitting at 2,700 feet in elevation, up into the pines above the 3,500 foot level. From there they can see the Drum Valley with Bear Mountain off in the distance.

Because of the terrain, horses must always walk during the trail rides. There is, however, a level spot near the lake, where riders can lope.

Other Activities

There are several other interesting activities for guests besides horseback riding. On Tuesdays, guests may take a motor trip into the two national parks nearby, Kings Canyon and Sequoia. The staff prepares bag lunches for the guests to take along.

More adventurous guests will enjoy the hike up a canyon to some underwater caves. To enter one of the caves, hikers must hold their heads and noses above the water. Once inside, they discover a large chamber. The entire excursion takes between two and three hours.

Down at the lake, guests can go fishing for blue gill and large mouth bass. Guests can also just relax by the M Bar J's 45-foot swimming pool. From the deck chairs, they have an unobstructed view of Big Baldy, an 8,209 foot mountain inside Kings Canyon National Park. There is also a heated spa near the pool.

Other activities include shuffleboard, ping pong, horseshoes, badminton, and volleyball. Evening entertainment includes square dancing and stargazing.

Archie Stockebrand, co-owner of M Bar J Guest Ranch, points out Native American Grinding holes

Accommodations

The M Bar J Guest Ranch has accommodations for 27 people. There are two-types of cabins at the ranch. The newer cinderblock buildings are modern and attractive, but lack the charm of the older wooden cabins with their flowered wallpaper and pine flooring.

A cabin for two adults is $95 a day or $570 a week, per person. Single occupancy is $105 a day or $630 a week. An additional child, eight to 12 years old, in the room is $40 a day or $240 a week. An additional child, two to seven years old, in the room is $20 a day or $120 week. Children under two are $12 a day or $72 a week.

Rooms with king- and queen-size beds are an additional $5 per day. A luxury two-bedroom motorhome is available for an additional $10 per day.

Dining

Everyone looks forward to meal times at the M Bar J. The food is delicious and there's plenty of it. Typical dinner entrees include turkey, lasagna, beef stew, fish, hamburgers, prime rib, and, of course, steak cooked personally by Archie.

Popular items like French toast, pancakes, and scrambled eggs show up on the breakfast menu, and lunches include pizza, turkey sandwiches, quiche, and grilled cheese sandwiches.

Horse Rental Rates

Horseback riding is included in the basic room rate.

Payment Method

The M Bar J Guest Ranch accepts cash, personal checks, traveler's checks, and American Express.

Rider Age Limit

Riders must be at least six years old.

Nearest Airport

The closest commercial airport is located in Visalia. However, private pilots may land at Woodlake.

How To Get There

From Visalia, take Highway 198 east. At Lemon Cove, go left on Highway 216 for a half mile. Just past the Kaweah River bridge, turn right on J-21. Follow J-21 for 18 miles. One mile before Badger, turn right on Stagecoach Drive. Go a half mile down the road. The ranch is on the left.

GRANT GROVE STABLES

Kings Canyon National Park
Grant Grove, CA 93633
No phone
Owner: D.R. Wilson

The giant sequoias in the Grant Grove area of Kings Canyon National Park are relatively few in number. There are many more white firs, incense cedars, sugar pines, and ponderosa pines around. But what the sequoias lack in numbers they more than make up for in size.

The General Grant Tree, which gives the grove its name, is the third largest living thing in the world. With a base diameter of 40.3 feet and a height equal to a 27-story building, it contains enough wood to build 40 five-room homes. Several of the other trees are also quite large.

For a close look at the trees, there is no substitute for old-fashioned foot power. But for exploring the area around the big trees, horseback is a great way to go. Grant Grove Stables, open from June through September, offers unscheduled rides on three different trails.

The choice for many vacationers is the one-hour ride that goes in a loop around the General Grant Tree. Leaving from the stables, riders head off north through the forest along a trail that goes up and down but never gains much elevation.

At one point, riders pass rustic Gamlin Cabin, which was originally built in 1872 by two brothers who made the area their home. The cabin was later used as a storage shed for the United States Cavalry and served as home for the first park ranger, Lewis L. Davis.

As the riders approach the General Grant Tree area, they half circle around it, getting as close as about 200 feet away. In all, there are 42 trees in the grove that have been specifically named, including one group of six trees called the Happy Family. Among the more famous sequoias is the General Robert E. Lee Tree, the 12th largest living thing in the world. Most of the other trees are named after states, including one named after the state of California. After viewing the grove from a distance, the riders return to the stables.

The one-and-a-half-hour ride may be the most scenic. The first part of the trip follows the same trail as the one-hour ride. It then branches off to the east. Along the way, riders cross Abbott Creek and head down to Round Meadow. At the meadow, which is filled with beautiful ferns, riders again cross Abbott Creek. Then they ride off into a forest of firs and pines, where they may spot a bear or deer wandering around. On their return to the stables, riders pass Crystal Spring Campground.

The longest ride at Grant Grove Stables takes two hours. Traveling through a forest of fir, pine, and a few unnamed sequoias, the group heads to the southern border of the park. Along the way, they cross

Sequoia Creek twice and pass the private community of Wilsonia. Eventually, the riders complete the loop and return to the stables.

One unusual feature of Grant Grove Stables is that it has no phone. To make a reservation, vacationers must go to the stables.

Traveling through the forest near Grant Grove Stables

Rates

The one-hour trail ride is $17. The one-and-a-half-hour ride is $25 and the two-hour ride is $30.

Payment Method

Grant Grove Stables accepts cash, personal checks with I.D., and traveler's checks.

Rider Age Limit

Riders must be at least five years old.

How To Get There

From the entrance to Kings Canyon National Park, take Highway 180 to Grant Grove. Then look for the sign to the pack station on the left.

CEDAR GROVE PACK STATION

P.O. Box 888
Kings Canyon National Park
Cedar Grove, CA 93633
(Winter Address)
P.O. Box 295
Three Rivers, CA 93271
(209) 561-3464 (Summer)
(209) 561-4621 (Winter)
Owner: Tim Loverin

Nowhere in North America have glaciers carved a deeper path through rugged mountain terrain than in Kings Canyon in the Sierra Nevada range. Deeper than Hell's Canyon in Idaho and the Grand Canyon in Arizona, mighty Kings Canyon reaches a depth of 8,200 feet at its lowest point.

As one might expect, Kings Canyon is an area that provides awesome views and spectacular scenery. It's also an area that can be explored by horseback. From May to October, Cedar Grove Pack Station, located in the heart of Kings Canyon National Park, offers trail rides that visit the surrounding region. Rides range in length from one hour to several days.

The one-hour and two-hour rides follow the South Fork Kings River upstream, allowing riders to observe this incredibly powerful river up close. At certain spots, rapids turn the entire river into a mass of white water, quite dangerous for anyone who ventures too close to the seething rapids. But for sightseers on horseback, this phenomenon is something to enjoy.

The scenery around the river is quite beautiful as well. The difference between the one-hour and two-hour rides is the turn-around point. Both trips, which come back along the same trail they take out, are quiet, peaceful rides along relatively flat terrain.

For more elevation gain, vacationers might consider the two-and-a-half-hour ride. From the pack station, riders head downstream briefly before turning up the Hotel Creek Trail. As the trail begins to climb, they can observe a small cascading waterfall on Hotel Creek. The trail then turns into a series of switchbacks, gaining 1,200 feet in elevation in about two miles. Wildflowers line the trail in the springtime. Other foliage along the way includes manzanita and live oak.

As they climb, riders go from hearing the sound of the river to hearing the wind in the trees. Eventually, they reach the top of a ridge and then proceed to an overlook point. From there they catch a panoramic view of Kings Canyon. The return is down the same trail.

The half-day trip follows the same trail up to the lookout. But then instead of returning down the trail, riders continue on the Lewis Creek Loop. They ride through a forest of yellow pines and then make a more gradual descent down to the river.

Tim Loverin, owner of Cedar Grove Pack Station, gives a hand up.

Riders have two choices for the all-day ride: They can either go to Bubbs Creek or Mist Falls. The trip to Mist Falls follows the Paradise Valley Trail, which runs along the South Fork Kings River. Along the way, riders pass waterfalls on Glacier Creek and Gardiner Creek. Upon reaching Mist Falls, they stop for lunch, and then return down the same trail.

The trip to Bubbs Creek begins six miles from the pack station at the end of the road. For a short distance, riders follow the Paradise Valley Trail. Then they cross the South Fork Kings River and head to the southeast, eventually crossing Bubbs Creek. A series of switchbacks follows. From the trail, riders have an excellent view of Kings Canyon. They also pass a prominent granite point called the Sphinx, which is 9,146 feet at its tip. At the top of the switchbacks, they move into a forest of firs and pine.

On some trips, riders will stop to take advantage of the excellent trout fishing. On other trips, they may continue all the way to Charlotte Creek for lunch. Particularly ambitious riders may even travel further on to Junction Meadow. All of these trips return down the same trail.

Cedar Grove Pack Station also offers extended trips into the back country. Some of the more popular destinations are East Lake, Woods Creek, and along Bubbs Creek to Viddette Meadow. Call or write Cedar Grove Pack Station for details about these longer trips.

Rates

The one-hour trail ride is $12.50 and the two-hour ride is $20. The two-and-a-half hour ride is $25 and the half-day trip is $40. The two all-day rides are both $50. All-inclusive back country trips range in price from $110 to $125 a day, per person. Extended trips, without a cook or food provided, are $80 per day for the guide and $35 per day for each pack animal.

Payment Method

Cedar Grove Pack Station accepts cash, personal checks, and traveler's checks.

Rider Age Limit

All riders must be at least five years old.

How To Get There

From the entrance to Kings Canyon National Park, take Highway 180 to Cedar Grove. Then look for the sign to the pack station.

WOLVERTON PACK STATION

P.O. Box 135
Sequoia National Park
California 93262
(209) 565-3445 (Summer)
(209) 564-2709 (Winter)
Owners: John & Sandy Vincent

HORSE CORRAL PACK STATION

P.O. Box 135
Sequoia National Park
California 93262
(Winter Address)
P.O. Box 641
Woodlake, CA 93286
(209) 565-3404 (Summer)
(209) 564-2709 (Winter)
Owners: The Vincents

After conservationist John Muir first encountered the giant redwoods in what is now Sequoia National Park, he remarked, "One naturally walked softly and awestruck among them." Such reverence is understandable, of course, when you consider that the sequoias in this area are the largest living things on earth.

In Sequoia National Park, vacationers can visit the trees on foot, of course. But they can also travel through the redwoods by horseback. From June through September, Wolverton Pack Station offers trail rides through groves of the great sequoias.

The most popular of these is the one-hour ride, offered five times each day at 9:00 a.m., 10:30 a.m., 1:00 p.m., 2:30 p.m., and 4:00 p.m. The simple, loop trail passes through a thick forest that contains not just redwoods, but also white firs, sugar firs, and a variety of other trees.

Occasionally, riders see bear, marmots, and deer as they ride along the trail. At one point, they go up Manzanita Mountain, where they have excellent mountain and valley views. Riders also have a view of the forest they don't get when they're down inside it. Specifically, they can see the tops of the sequoias poking up above the other trees. Eventually, the loop brings them back to the pack station.

The two-hour ride, which is offered at 8:30 a.m. and 2:30 p.m., heads up into the Wolverton Ski Area. From the parking lot above the ski area, riders travel south along the edge of Long Meadow. The meadow, which is surrounded by fir trees, fills up with wildflowers in the summer. After a heavy winter, snow sometimes stays on the ground in places right through June.

At the end of the meadow, riders head down a series of switchbacks to the Alta Trail, a portion of the ride that takes about 15 minutes. From the Alta Trail, they connect up with the same trail used for the one-hour trip, which passes through the sequoias. Eventually, this trail brings them back to the pack station.

Once each day at 8:30 a.m., Wolverton Pack Station wranglers lead a half-day ride. The first portion of the trip is along a series of gravel ridges. The crushed rock in these ridges was created by ancient glaciers that moved through the canyon. Farther up the trail, riders enter a thick forest of red fir.

Eventually, they reach Panther Gap at an elevation of 8,450 feet. Looking off to the south, riders can see the Kaweah River some 5,000 feet below. Off to the east and southeast, they can see the high peaks of the Great Western Divide. From Panther Gap, riders go west along the Alta Trail, which provides an excellent view of Panther Peak. The trail takes them down below Long Meadow and then back to the pack station.

Pack Trips

The owners of Wolverton Pack Station also operate Horse Corral Pack Station in the Horse Corral Meadow area of Sequoia National Park.

They arrange spot, extended, and all-inclusive trips throughout the park. Among the more popular destinations are Deadman Canyon, Cloud Canyon, the Five Lakes region, the Nine Lakes basin, Big Arroyo, and the Kern River.

Rates

The one-hour trail ride is $12 and the two-hour ride is $20. The half-day trip is $35. One-day spot trips from Horse Corral Pack Station are $40 per day for horses and mules. Longer spot trips are $30 per day for horses and mules. Extended trips are $30 per day for horses and mules. Packers are $60 per day and cooks are $60 per day. All-inclusive trips for groups of four or fewer people are $125 a person per day. The rate for groups of five or more is $110 a person per day.

Payment Method

Wolverton Pack Station and Horse Corral Pack Station accept cash, personal checks from California Banks, and traveler's checks.

Rider Age Limit

Riders must be at least seven years old; however, exceptions will be made for big, strong five and six year olds.

How To Get There

From the entrance to Sequoia National Park at Ash Mountain, take Highway 198 through the Giant Forest Village. A mile past the turn-off for the General Sherman Tree, turn right on the road to Wolverton Ski Area. Drive a short way up the road and turn right. Then follow the road to Wolverton Pack Station.

To reach Horse Corral Pack Station, continue along Highway 198 past the Wolverton turn-off. Turn right at the sign for Big Meadow Camp Ground. Go all the way to the end of the road to Horse Corral Meadow.

MINERAL KING PACK STATION

P.O. Box 61
Three Rivers, CA 93271
(209) 561-3404 (Summer)
(209) 561-4142 (Winter)
Owner: Don Bedell

There are 698 curves, many of them hairpin, on the 25 mile road to Mineral King. Originally constructed in 1879, the narrow, sometimes unpaved road, which the park service describes as "tortuous," discourages many potential visitors. Those who are more adventurous, however, are richly rewarded.

Mineral King, once the site of several unsuccessful silver mines, is without question the most beautiful area accessible by car in all of the Southern Sierras. Sitting in a bowl at 7,500 feet elevation, this high mountain valley has a distinctive alpine character. Spectacular mountain peaks, some snow-capped even in the summertime, surround Mineral King.

But you don't have to settle for just a view from a distance. Mineral King Pack Station, open from mid-June to mid-September, offers a number of trail rides that go right up into the mountains. The trips range in length from two hours to two weeks.

For the vacationer interested in a short ride with great mountain views, Mineral King Pack Station offers two different two-hour rides. One heads off in a northerly direction along the Monarch Lakes Trail. As the trip begins, riders pass Black Wolf Falls on the right. The trail then climbs in a series of switchbacks, gaining elevation quite rapidly. In one mile, the trail goes up 920 vertical feet.

Eventually, riders reach Ground Hog Meadow, which was named for the many yellow-bellied marmots that scurry about. It's a beautiful spot, particularly in the summer when the wildflowers are in bloom. Nearby on Monarch Creek, a waterfall cascades down. From Ground Hog Meadow, riders have a panoramic view of the Mineral King Valley and the mountain peaks above. After enjoying the view, it's a ride back to the stables.

The alternative two-hour ride heads up the Franklin Lakes Trail. The early part of the trail follows a road, no longer open to vehicles, that leads to Aspen Flat. At Crystal Creek, the trail begins to climb more rapidly and the vegetation changes. Manzanita, ceanothus, and an occasional juniper are seen along the trail. The riders reach a meadow near Franklin Creek, where they encounter a mountain waterfall. Looking back across the valley, they can see Sawtooth Peak rising up 12,393 feet. They then return down the same trail.

The short trip that most people consider the most scenic is the half-day ride up the White Chief Trail. Leaving Mineral King Pack Station, riders cross Spring Creek, which comes right out of the side of the mountain to form a waterfall. Then it's on up a trail that runs somewhat parallel to the Franklin Lakes Trail, ascending rather steadily. The trail becomes steeper as it comes up through a canyon.

Eventually, riders reach a breathtaking alpine meadow at the 9,600 foot level, which in the summer is full of colorful wildflowers. Looking back to the north, they can spot a number of prominent sights, including Timber Gap and Empire Mountain. The group then returns down the same trail. The entire trip is about three and a half hours.

There is also a longer half-day trip, about four and a half hours in length, up to Mosquito Lake #1. Riders follow the White Chief Trail for a mile before heading off to the west on a separate route. They climb over Miner's Ridge and then drop down to the lake, which is surrounded by red fir. The group stops for lunch and then returns back down the mountain.

Riders are given options for the full-day trip. They can choose to ride to either Monarch Lake, Crystal Lake or Cobalt Lake for some fishing. Or they can spend all day in the saddle and ride to the top of Franklin Pass. On the fishing trips, riders can expect to spend five to six hours in the saddle. They spend the balance of the time fishing.

The trip to Franklin Pass is a tough eight-hour grind with a 3,500 foot elevation gain. The reward for all this work is an unbelievable view from on top of the Great Western Divide at 11,760 feet elevation. There is something to see in almost every direction,.with Mount Whitney as the highlight.

Pack Trips

Mineral King Pack Station also offers a number of extended trips that can range from three to 14 days. The choice of destination is up to the rider. Generally, the trips are in loops and they use all the major passes leading out of Mineral King. Some explore the Five Lakes Basin. Others go up into the Great Western Divide. Still others come into the Kern River Canyon.

Riders can choose to do their own cooking or they can select a trip that includes a cook. There are special trips intended primarily for photographers and other trips that cater to those who enjoy fly fishing.

Spot pack trips are available as well. Among the most common destinations are Rattlesnake Creek, Cliff Creek, Little Kern River, and Hockett Meadows.

Additional Facilities

The owners of Mineral King Pack Station recently took over control of Kennedy Meadows Pack Trains, which operates at the southern end of the eastern Sierra. At the new facility, they're offering spot trips to the Kern Plateau, Big Kern River, and Domeland Wilderness. Anglers, in particular, will be interested in the outstanding golden trout fishing available in this part of the Sierra. Write or call Mineral King Pack Station for more information.

Horse Drives

The most exciting new features offered by Kennedy Meadows Pack Trains are the spring and fall horse drives. This is particularly good news for trail riders from southern California, because now they don't have to drive as far to enjoy a horse drive.

The three-day spring drive begins at Walker Pass. Wranglers move the horses up through Chimney Creek Canyon, where the group stops for the first night. Picking up the Pacific Crest Trail on the second day, they travel to a camping spot at Kennedy Meadows. On the final day, they drive the horses up to the pack station at Black Rock Trailhead.

In the fall, at the end of the packing season, they drive the horses back down to Walker Pass.

Rates

The two-hour trail ride is $30. The half-day trip on the White Chief Trail is $37 and the half-day trip to Mosquito Lake #1 is $42. The full-day fishing trips are $50 and the full-day trip to Franklin Pass is $60.

The longer all-inclusive trips are $130 a day per person for five days or more and $140 a day per person for four days or less. When cooking and gear are not included in the package, the charge is $95 a day per person for five days or more and $100 a day per person for four days or less. The total charge for spot pack trips range from $200 to $400 per person, depending upon the number of people in a group and the destination.

The three-day horse drives are $210.

Payment Method

Mineral King Pack Station accepts cash, personal checks, and traveler's checks.

Rider Age Limit

Riders must be at least six years old for day rides and seven years old for pack trips. No doubling is permitted.

How To Get There

From Highway 198 at Three Rivers, head east on Mineral King Road. Continue down the road for 25 miles. Mineral King Pack Station is at the end of the road on the left.

SHANNON RANCH

Rt. 4, Box 107
Porterville, CA 93257
(209) 535-4543
Owner: Jack & Sandi Shannon

GOLDEN TROUT WILDERNESS PACKTRAINS

P.O. Box 756
Springville, CA 93265
(209) 542-2816 (Summer)
(209) 539-2744 (Winter)
Owner: Dan Shew

Anyone who has ever watched Howard Hawk's movie classic *Red River* or read Larry McMurtry's best seller *Lonesome Dove* is familiar with the spectacle and romance of an old-fashioned cattle drive.

What people are now discovering, of course, is that cattle drives are more than mere celluloid fantasies. Even in the 1990s, they are still the best way to move cattle to better grazing land. And what makes them appealing to trail riders is that you don't have to be a full-time cowboy to join in the fun.

The Shannon Ranch, located near Deer Creek in the foothills of the southern Sierra, runs cattle drives during the spring and the fall, and vacationers can be part of the crew.

It's no easy job, of course. Riders spend long hours in the saddle keeping track of the herd. But for most people, it's the experience of a lifetime. They get to ride through some of the most beautiful country in the world, eat western-style food around a camp fire, and sleep out under the stars.

Throughout the trip, everything needed, except a sleeping bag and personal gear, is provided, and the drives are expertly led by wranglers from Golden Trout Wilderness Packtrains.

The spring drive begins at the ranch in early June. For the first two days, riders help the cowboys round up all the cattle. Then, with cowboys shouting and the cattle bawling, they hit the trail. Heading north along a trail that was first established by Reuben Shannon in 1918, riders and cattle quickly begin gaining elevation. From a starting elevation of 700 feet, they move up over 6,000 feet in relatively short order and then drop down slightly as they pass through Long Meadow.

Continuing north at a rate of about ten miles a day, the cattle drive moves through thick forests of fir and pine. At one point, riders pass one of the major sights in the region, the massive monolith of granite called Dome Rock. The drive moves through Quaking Aspen, Lloyd Meadow, and across Fish Creek Ridge. Finally, after five days, riders and cattle descend on Grey Meadow, which serves as the summer home for the herd.

During the summer, the calves put on several hundred pounds eating the high mountain grass. Then in mid-September, Shannon Ranch conducts a second drive to return the cattle to lower elevations for the winter. Again, the cattle have to be rounded up. The drive then leads down the same trail that was followed in the spring. In all, riders spend six days gathering the cattle and riding with them back to Shannon Ranch. They spend one additional day before the drive getting to Grey Meadow.

Pack Trips

When the experienced cowpokes from Golden Trout Wilderness Packtrains aren't out driving cattle, they're busy arranging spot, extended, and all-inclusive trips into the Golden Trout Wilderness region. Among the more popular destinations are Funston Meadow, Little Whitney Meadows, Coyote Lakes, Kern Hot Springs, and Maggie Lakes.

Their most ambitious trip, however, is to Mount Whitney. Riders can make it by horseback to within two miles of the top of the highest mountain in the contiguous 48 states. From there, they complete the climb by foot. The loop trip to Mount Whitney takes ten days to complete, but guarantees unforgettable memories.

Rates

The charge for two days of gather and the five day cattle drive is $995. Participation in two days of gather and one day of the cattle drive is $450. Participation in three days of the cattle drive is $450.

Spot trips arranged by Golden Trout Packtrains are $35 a day per animal and $95 a day per packer. Extended trips are $30 a day per animal and $85 a day per packer. All-inclusive pack trips are $120 a day per person for groups of six.

Payment Method

Shannon Ranch and Golden Trout Wilderness Packtrains accept only cash, personal checks, and traveler's checks.

Rider Age Limit

For the cattle drive, riders must be at least 16 years old with some horse experience and must be accompanied by their parents. There are no limits on riders 18 and over. Golden Trout Wilderness Packtrains has no age limit for its pack trips.

How To Get There

Directions to Shannon Ranch will be provided to participants after they are signed up for a drive.

To reach Golden Trout Wilderness Packtrains, take Highway 190 from Porterville. Follow it left, just past Pierpoint Spurs. Then continue to Quaking Aspen Camp Ground. At the campground, turn left and look for signs to the pack station.

BALCH PARK PACK STATION

P.O. Box 852
Springville, CA 93265
(209) 539-2227 (Summer)
(209) 539-3908 (Winter)
Owner: Tim and Dianne Shew

When people think of the best places in California to see giant redwoods, the areas that usually come to mind are national parks like Sequoia, Kings Canyon, and Yosemite. But there are other places in the Sierras, which few have ever seen, with spectacular groves of sequoias.

One of the most beautiful is Balch Park, located just a few miles outside the southern boundary of Sequoia National Park. Tucked inside Mountain Home State Forest at a 6,500 feet elevation, Balch Park is a place where vacationers can enjoy exceptional scenery without having to rub elbows with the tourist hordes.

They can also enjoy it by horseback. Balch Park Pack Station offers half-day and full-day trail rides that go through the forests nearby, and extended trips that go into the back country.

On the half-day trip, riders go to Hidden Falls and return. Traveling along trails that are shaded by giant sequoias, riders drop down to the Middle Fork of the Tule River, where they can view the falls. As the name suggests, the falls are somewhat difficult to see. But from the right spot, riders have an excellent view. Continuing from Hidden Falls, they cross the river at Redwood Crossing and then return by way of the Eastside Trail. Throughout the trip, which lasts about three and a half hours, the horses always walk.

There are two choices for the full-day ride. Those who like to combine fishing with riding can go down to Tule River for fishing and then up to Strawberry Meadow for lunch. On this trip, the wrangler brings along an extra pack animal to carry the food. Generally, riders can expect to spend about four hours in the saddle and the balance of the day fishing and relaxing.

The other option is to ride up to Summit Lake, which is a much tougher trip. It takes approximately three and a half hours to get there and a good three hours to get back. When riders reach the lake, however, they are treated to a spectacular view. From the lake, which sits on the border of Sequoia National Park at 9,400 feet elevation, they have a panoramic view of the Sierra high country. Among the sights are Maggie Peak and Moses Peak.

There are even more choices available to riders for the extended trips. Virtually any lake, stream, or wilderness destination within a few days riding distance from the pack station can be part of a trip. One of the most popular destinations for a two-day trip is the Maggie Lakes area.

For longer trips, riders usually choose Southfork Meadow, Twin Lakes, or Summit Lake, where they establish a base camp. From the base camp, they take day trips for fishing or sightseeing. The most popular base camp is Southfork Meadow, which acquired its name from the river that passes through it, the Southfork of the Kaweah River. From Southfork Meadow, riders can easily reach Blossom Lakes, Hockett Lakes, and several nearby meadows

Rates

The half-day ride is $25 per person. All-day rides are $40 per person. On the all-day ride, a pack horse is included to carry lunch. Lunch is provided by the rider. All-inclusive trips are available for two, three, and five days for minimum groups of four. The two-day trip is $150 per person, the three-day trip is $285 per person, and the five-day trip is $475 per person. Everything is provided on the all-inclusive trips except a sleeping bag.

Trips are also available for riders who prefer to do their own cooking. A guide with a horse is $70 a day for extended trips and $85 for spot trips. Horses and mules are $25 a day each for extended trips and $35 a day each for spot trips.

Payment Method

Balch Park Pack Station prefers cash, but will also accept personal checks or traveler's checks.

Rider Age Limit

There is no age limit and youngsters may double with their parents.

How To Get There

From Highway 99, head east on Highway 190. Just outside Springville, take J37 north. Turn right at Bear Creek Road. Then turn right on Balch Park Road. Look for the signs for the Balch Park Pack Station.

The Hunewell Ranch wranglers

The main residence at Hunewill ranch hidden behind the poplars.

EASTERN SIERRA 10

HUNEWILL CIRCLE H GUEST RANCH

P.O. Box 368
Bridgeport, CA 93517
(619) 932-7710 (Summer)
(702) 465-2201 (Winter)
(702) 465-2325 (Winter)
Owner: Lenore Hunewill

It was the Gold Rush that brought Napoleon Bonaparte Hunewill to California back in 1852, and it was prospecting in the Mother Lode that made him a wealthy man. But it isn't gold mining or even his later involvement with the lumber industry that are his most enduring legacy. It is the magnificent ranch he started in the Bridgeport Valley in 1861 that carries the Hunewill name right down to the present day.

Now, more than 130 years later, this 5,000-acre spread in the Eastern Sierra, has become one of the most highly-regarded guest ranches in the country, with good reason. The setting–lush, green pasture land with jagged Sawtooth Ridge as a backdrop–is perfect. The members of the Hunewill family, particularly matriarch Lenore Hunewill, are delightful. And the activities at the ranch are tremendous fun.

It is not, however, a resort. Vacationers looking for swimming pools and golf courses would be better served elsewhere. But for those seeking a more traditional ranch experience with plenty of old-fashioned warmth and country hospitality, the Hunewill Ranch, open from May through September, is hard to beat.

As one might expect on a ranch with over 2,000 head of cattle, horseback riding is the number one activity. When the cattle need gathering or moving, guests are invited to join in. The rest of the time, they can participate in a variety of riding activities that have been organized by ability group–beginning, intermediate, and advanced.

Less experienced riders can learn basic riding skills in the safe surroundings of the nearby pastures, while more advanced riders can lope across the wide-open fields of the huge ranch without restraint. On other occasions, they might ride over to the entrance of either Buckeye Canyon or Robinson Canyon and then return. Typically, a riding session is scheduled each morning and afternoon, except on Wednesdays.

On Wednesday's, guests can go on a day ride to one of several destinations. Sometimes, they follow the creek up Buckeye Canyon, site of N.B. Hunewill's sawmill operation, all the way to Buckeye Forks, near the Yosemite National Park border. From the ranch sitting at 6,500 feet in elevation, they make roughly a 2,000 foot climb. Other times, they take the trail that follows Eagle Creek up from Buckeye Canyon towards Eagle Peak and Robinson Peak to above the 10,000 foot level.

For a different alternative, riders climb up to 10,126 foot high Rickey Peak to the north of Buckeye Canyon. Or they follow Tamarack Creek up to Tamarack Lake and then to Hunewill Lake, just below the Crater Crest at over 10,000 feet in elevation.

Cattle Drive

Those looking for an even more adventurous riding experience, might consider the Hunewill Ranch's fall cattle drive, which has a rather unique feature. Rather than having to sleep on the ground during the five-day drive, riders are brought back to the ranch each night so that they can enjoy the comforts of a bed. Between 15 and 20 guests can participate in the drive, normally conducted during the first week in November each year.

Following essentially the same route that the Hunewills have used since 1911, the group crosses Highway 395, with a helpful assist from the California Highway Patrol. Then they travel through the Bridgeport Valley, past the Bridgeport Reservoir, and down Walker Canyon.

The group continues up over 7,200 foot high Sweetwater Summit and down into the winter grazing lands of the Smith Valley in Nevada. On the last night of the drive, the group all gathers for a final dinner at the Heyday Restaurant in Wellington, Nevada.

Other Activities

When guests aren't out on the range, they can relax with a game of volleyball, ping pong, or horseshoes. If they're feeling a little saddle sore, they can take a day hike or do some fishing in one of the nearby canyons. Or they can go off to hit a few tennis balls on the public courts in Bridgeport. They can also take a sidetrip by car to the historic ghost town of Bodie, roughly 25 miles away.

There are a number of activities available in the evenings as well. Guests get to polish up their allemande lefts and do-si-dos on square dance night. They can do a little singing under the open sky on hayride night. And they can ham it up on skit night with help from the staff.

On Sundays, the Hunewill Ranch organizes a barbecue dinner over at the Buckeye Creek cookout area and on Friday nights a second barbecue is held up at the Robinson Creek cookout area. Guests are asked to drive their automobiles to both of these events.

On Tuesday mornings, guests mount up early and ride over to Robinson Creek for a hearty cowboy breakfast of pancakes, eggs, bacon, and coffee.

Accommodations

In keeping with the spirit of the ranch, the guest facilities are simple, but comfortable. Guests can either stay in the old two-story Colonial ranch house, built back in 1880, or in one of the nearby guest cottages. In all, up to 50 guests can be accommodated for a week's stay, though typically the number ranges from 45 to 49.

The ranch house has two rooms available with two twin beds in each and a connecting bath. The rates range from $660 per person to $720 per person, depending upon the time of season. Rates for singles range from $706 to $766.

The older, brown, wood-sided cottages have two rooms each, a covered front porch, and no connecting door. Each room in the cottage has a private bath and two twin beds. The rates range from $688 per person to $748 per person. Rates for singles range from $723 to $783.

The newer, white, wood-sided cottages have two rooms each, a covered porch, and a connecting door, if needed. Each room in the cottage has a private bath and two twin beds. The rates range from $717 per person to $777 per person. Rates for singles range from $775 to $835.

Discounts are available for a third person in a room on a roll-away bed, for children under 10, and for children under two.

Dining

The quality of the meals at the Hunewill Ranch is something on which the family and staff prides itself. Guests are treated to delectable fish, chicken, beef, and pork entrees. Of course, only top-grade, grain-fed beef raised right there at the ranch is served. Special care is taken to accommodate those guests on special and low-fat diets.

Horse Rental Rates

The basic room rate includes the use of a saddle horse during the stay at the ranch. The five-day cattle drive is $549, including meals and lodging.

Payment Method

The Hunewill Ranch accepts cash, personal checks, and traveler's checks.

Rider Age Limit

All riders must be at least six years old. Children between six and ten years old may participate in the "Little Buckaroo" riding program. A resident baby-sitter is available to look after smaller children.

Nearest Airport

The closest commercial airport is located in Reno, Nevada. Private pilots, however, may fly into Bridgeport.

How To Get There

From Reno or Lake Tahoe, head south on Highway 395. From southern California, head north on Highway 395. At Bridgeport, take the Twin Lakes turn-off. Proceed five miles down the road and look for the Hunewill Ranch sign.

VIRGINIA LAKES PACK OUTFIT

H.C. Route 1, Box 1070
Bridgeport, CA 93517
(619) 937-0326 (Summer)
(702) 867-2591 (Winter)
Owners: Tom and Martha Roberts

There was a time centuries ago when the northeast corner of what today is Yosemite National Park, had many regular visitors. Paiute Indians from Mono Lake would travel through this rugged countryside every summer on their way to Tuolumne Meadows for trading sessions with the Awahneeche Indians.

But in more recent times, it has become the area in the park that receives the fewest visitors. Far from any highway, it's considered too inaccessible. There is, however, a way that vacationers can enjoy the untouched beauty of the alpine lakes, hidden valleys, and towering peaks that dot this remote corner of the park.

Virginia Lakes Pack Outfit, located six miles west of Highway 395 between Lee Vining and Bridgeport, offers trail rides that go into the heart of the Yosemite backcountry. They also conduct shorter trips through the Hoover Wilderness Area, just east of the national park border.

The shortest of these is the two-hour trip. On this brief journey through the nearby red shale country, riders travel up to Blue Lake, Cooney Lakes, and Frog Lakes. The trip, which gains 1,500 feet in elevation is basically up and back.

For an easier two-hour trip, riders can travel over to Green Lake and back. The lake, which sits at 8,900 feet in elevation, is actually at a slightly lower elevation than the pack station, but it provides some excellent views. Riders can see Bridgeport, Mono Lake, and the historic town of Bodie off in the distance.

Riders who like to fish might consider the half-day trip. Following the same trail used for the first two-hour trip, they make the climb to Frog Lakes. After arriving, they have time to eat lunch and do a little fishing, before returning back to the pack station. The whole trip lasts about four hours.

The all-day trip is also appealing to fishermen. Starting out along a trail that winds around past the Virginia Lakes, riders climb up to Summit Lake, which is right on the national park border. Sitting in the shadow of Camiaca Peak, the 10,160 foot high lake offers a beautiful setting for fishing.

Pack Trips

The most interesting trips, however, are the ones that actually go inside Yosemite National Park. Virginia Lakes Pack Outfit conducts custom, all-inclusive trips to a number of spots in the northeast corner of the park. Among the more popular destinations are Miller Lake, Smedburg Lake, and Benson Lake.

Benson Lake, in particular, has developed a reputation among riders as a great place to visit. Located at the relatively low elevation of 7,560 feet, the lake has a long sandy beach, known as the "Riviera of the Sierra," that is great for sunbathing. Swimming is also possible. Though chilly, the lake is a few degrees warmer than others in the region.

Regardless of which destination is selected, one of the highlights of the deluxe all-expense trips are the gourmet meals, including Beef Wellington, that Martha Roberts plans.

The custom, all-inclusive trips are arranged for private groups containing two or more people. There is a second option for vacationers that is more economical, though less private. Virginia Lakes Pack Outfit schedules several group trips each summer. Vacationers can sign up to be part of an eight-person group. As with the private trips, wranglers do the cooking and camp chores. Instead of Beef Wellington, however, riders can expect slightly less fancy meals. Orange Roughy, Chicken Dijon, and Vegetarian Lasagna are typical of the entrees offered on the group trips.

The shortest of the trips is four days long. Vacationers ride off to a base camp in the wilderness, where they stay for three nights. The pack station staff prepares all meals and performs all camp chores. The horses, however, do not remain at the camp. They leave and come back on the fourth day for the ride out. In the meantime, vacationers can fish, hike, read, take pictures or just relax.

Vacationers who would like to ride more might prefer the five-day trip to a base camp in Yosemite National Park. As with the four-day trip, all meals and chores are included. The difference is that vacationers have the use of a horse throughout the five days.

More adventurous vacationers will prefer the seven-day trip. Instead of setting up at a base camp, the group travels to different locations, allowing visitors to explore all over the northeast corner of Yosemite National Park.

Virginia Lakes Pack Outfit also offers spot trips and extended trips for riders who prefer to do all their own cooking and chores.

Rates

The two-hour ride is $25 and the half-day ride is $35. The all-day ride is $50. Spot trips are $275 per person for parties of two and $255 per person for parties of three or more. Extended trips are $100 per day for the packer and $50 per day for each horse or mule. All-expense trips are $190 a day per person for parties of two. Parties of three or four are $165 a day per person. Parties of five or more are $145 a day per person. The package price for the scheduled four-day all-expense base camp trip is $260 per person. The five-day all-expense base camp trip is $400 per person. The seven-day all-expense traveling trip is $660 per person.

Payment Method

Virginia Lake Pack Outfit accepts cash, personal checks, traveler's checks, and America Express.

Rider Age Limit

Riders must be at least six years old.

How To Get There

Leave Highway 395 just 13 miles south of Bridgeport, or 13 miles north of Lee Vining, at Conway Summit. Travel six miles west and look for the sign on the right hand side. Take the dirt road up to the pack station.

FRONTIER PACK TRAIN

Star Route 3, Box 18
June Lake, CA 93529
(619) 648-7701 (Summer)
(619) 387-2635 (Winter)
Owner: Dink Getty

For more than three-quarters of a century, the June Lakes Loop in the Eastern Sierra has been a popular resort destination. In the early years, Hollywood celebrities, ex-President Herbert Hoover, and others made the trek to this scenic locale that was famous even then for its fishing.

These days, vacationers come to the June Lakes Loop, just north of Mammoth Lakes, not only to fish, but to hike, camp, and, in the wintertime, ski. If they're dedicated trail riders, of course, they also come for another reason – to experience the exceptional beauty of the June Lakes region by horseback.

Frontier Pack Train, located across from Silver Lake on the June Lakes Loop, offers short excursions and extended expeditions from June through early October each year.

The shortest of these is a one-hour ride through the sagebrush and along Rush Creek that departs five times each day at 9:00 a.m., 10:30 a.m., 1:00 p.m., 2:30 p.m., and 4:00 p.m. This trip will appeal primarily to first-time riders and younger children who can double up with parents. Aside from the pleasant scenery along the June Lakes Loop and the invigorating mountain air, the ride has little to offer.

The half-day trip is a bit more challenging. Riders leave twice a day–8:30 a.m. and 1:00 p.m.–along a trail that swings past a small waterfall, before climbing up through the sagebrush to the top of Parker Bench. Looking off to the east, riders have an outstanding view of Mono Lake and Mono Craters. After enjoying the view and exploring the site of an old mining camp, they take the trail back down to the pack station.

More ambitious riders might consider the all-day trip that goes up into the Ansel Adams Wilderness. Departing once a day at 7:30 a.m., riders take a trail that goes up past Agnew Lake and over to Gem Lake, where they spend the day fishing, swimming, or relaxing. In the afternoon, they return along the same route, descending over 1,800 feet back down to Silver Lake.

Pack Trips

Early in the season, the pack station conducts five-day trips into the back country that are specifically designed for fly fishermen. A second set of fishing trips is offered from Labor Day through early October. Each of the trips, which are limited to ten people, are led by well-known fly-fishing experts like Ralph Cutter, who are available for tips and guidance.

Leaving from the pack station at Silver Lake, riders begin their five-day fishing vacation by climbing up into Ansel Adams Wilderness. Camp for the first two nights is established on a bluff overlooking a meadow near Clark Lakes. The balance of the first day is spent fishing for brook trout.

On the second day, riders head up to Thousand Island Lake, the headwaters of the San Joaquin River. Surrounded by a starkly beautiful alpine landscape and dominated by 12,945 foot high Banner Peak, the lake is dotted with the small, tree-covered islands that inspired its name. Riders spend several hours fishing for a rainbow-golden trout hybrid before returning to Clark Lakes.

The following morning, they head off for Alger Lakes. As they cross 10,700 foot Gem Pass, riders have a spectacular view across the border into Nevada to the east. Looking back to the west, they catch a sweeping view of the jagged peaks that dominate the Ritter Range. They then drop down into the Alger Lakes basin. Mt. Wood, Parker Peak, Koip Peak, and

Blacktop Peak, standing in a ring around the lakes, provide a dramatic setting for riders as they fish for trophy-sized golden trout on a catch-and-release basis.

The fourth day and fifth morning are spent at the lake. Then everyone saddles up and heads back to the pack station.

During the month of July, the pack station offers a four-day base camp trip to Clark Lakes that is intended for families. During their stay at the camp, family members can relax, hike, fish, or take optional day rides. One of the day trips goes over to Thousand Island Lake. Another goes up to the top of Carson Peak, where riders can look down on the June Lakes Loop area. All meals throughout the trip are provided.

The premier rides offered by Frontier Pack Train, however, are the five-day trips from the June Lakes area through the spectacular high country of Yosemite National Park to Tuolumne Meadows. Seven trips, limited to 10 people each, are offered every summer. Of the seven, some are private trips and some are open. All follow the same route and include meals like steak, home-made lasagna, and steak and chicken kabobs.

On the first day, riders follow the trail up to Gem Lake and then continue on past Waugh Lake to Marie Meadow. The next morning, they take a day trip over to Davis Lakes for fishing, sightseeing, or relaxing. On the third day, riders go up over 11,056 foot high Donohue Pass and enter Yosemite National Park. Continuing along the John Muir Trail, riders catch a view of the highest peak in Yosemite, 13,144 foot high Mt. Lyell, and below it, the largest glacier in the Sierra, Lyell Glacier.

Upon reaching the fork of Kuna Creek and Lyell Fork, a second camp is established in a lush meadow surrounded by trees. The following day, riders take a side trip to Vogelsang, one of the more popular high country destinations. On the fifth day, they ride out to Tuolumne Meadows. Transportation is then provided back to the pack station at June Lakes.

Frontier Pack Train also arranges custom trips for groups of six or more people for anywhere in the wilderness they want to go.

During the winter time, Frontier Pack Train moves its operation to the Millpond Riding and Roping Center near Bishop, where trail rides into the Sierra foothills are offered.

Cattle Drives

Frontier Pack Train offers an interesting alternative to the typical cattle drive for city slickers who prefer a faster pace. Instead of a slow-moving herd of cows and calves, they drive faster-moving yearlings in two groups of a 100 head each. The three-day spring drives take place during the first and last weeks of May. The fall drives take place in early September and early October.

Between 30 and 40 guests join 14 wranglers to handle the drive. The level of active participation is up to each guest. They can either join right in with the wranglers or hang back in the rear and enjoy the ride. The downside of hanging back, of course, is that the riders in the rear eat the most dust.

Before each drive begins, riders participate in an informal class on how to herd cattle. It's a practical football-style chalk board session that covers topics like how not to break up a herd. The cattle drive class is followed by an old-fashioned barbecue.

The following morning, riders hit the trail. Leaving from Mill Pond, the drive travels north through the Pleasant Valley area and up into the Inyo National Forest. The first night, the group camps at the base of Casa Diablo Mountain. The second day, they continue north to Moran Spring, where they spend the night.

On the third day, they travel through Wildrose Canyon and then on up to a spot just above Black Lake, where they spend their final night. The area around Black Lake serves as grazing land for the cattle during the summer. Then in the fall, they are driven along the same route back to Mill Pond.

Horse Drives

Frontier Pack Train is one of several pack outfits that offers a horse drive at the beginning and the end of each season. For many riders, this is the most exciting event they can participate in all year, because it truly tests their riding skills. Instead of walking along a trail, riders get to run with the horses across open territory. Often, the biggest challenge is simply trying to hold them back. Roughly 50 riders participate in each drive, which for many is the thrill of a lifetime.

For the spring drive, riders meet at the pack station at June Lake. From there, they are taken by bus to Benton, a spot due east of Black Lake, where the trip begins.

Once under way, the drive heads west into the Inyo National Forest to a spot called Wet Meadow, where they stop for the first night. On the second day, they travel along a ridge that overlooks Long Meadow, before stopping for the night at East Crater Sand Flat in the Mono Craters area. The following day, they cross Mono Craters, go past Reverse Peak, and come down by Grant Lake into the June Lake Loop area.

The fall drive in October, basically goes in the reverse direction.

Wild Mustang Trips

Frontier Pack Train is one of two pack outfits in the Eastern Sierra that takes riders on expeditions to view wild mustangs. Of all the trips, this is the one that offers riders the most freedom. They don't have to travel in a single-file line and their pace isn't set by independently-minded cows or horses.

The three-day trips are offered during April and May on Fridays, Saturdays and Sundays. Riders meet at Millpond Riding and Roping, where they are provided with transportation to the base camp.

From the base camp at Truman Meadows, riders travel through the Montgomery Pass Wild Horse Territory to observe a herd of approximately 300 wild mustangs. The high desert landscape in this area is dotted with pinon pine and sagebrush. As riders follow the mustangs through the wilds, they have ample opportunity to capture great photographs. They may even witness a mare foaling. Among the other animals frequently encountered in the region are deer and pronghorn antelope.

Back at the base camp, riders are treated to hearty meals and western-style entertainment around a campfire. On Sunday afternoon, they are transported back to Millpond.

Rates

The one-hour ride is $15 per person or $20 for a child doubled with a parent. The half-day ride is $35 and the all-day ride is $50. The five-day fly fishing trip is $650 per person. The four-day base camp trip to Clark Lakes is $440 per person. The five-day trip to Tuolumne Meadows is $675. The cattle drive is $450 and the horse drive is $270. The three-day trip to view wild mustangs is $270.

Payment Method

Frontier Pack Train accepts cash, personal checks, and traveler's checks.

Rider Age Limit

Riders must be at least six years old for the day trips and eight years old for the pack trips. Youngsters from one-and-a-half to six may double with a parent on the one-hour ride only.

How To Get There

To get to Frontier Pack Train, take Highway 395 north from Bishop or south from Lee Vining. From Highway 395, take the June Lake Loop turnoff. Follow the road for seven miles and look for the pack station across from Silver Lake.

To get to Millpond Riding and Roping, take Highway 395 north from Bishop. Five miles north of Bishop, turn off on Ed Powers Road. Go a quarter mile and turn right on Sawmill Road. Proceed down Sawmill Road and look for Millpond Riding and Roping on the left.

MAMMOTH LAKES PACK OUTFIT

P.O. Box 61
Mammoth Lakes, CA 93546
(619) 934-2434
Owners: Lou and Mary Roeser

It's hard to say exactly when the first pack train began operating in the Mammoth Lakes region. But by the time the mining boom of the late 1870s was in full swing, pack animals were regularly traveling over Mammoth Pass on their way to and from the western side.

Eventually, the mining activity diminished, but it was replaced by an industry that has proved infinitely more lucrative for this isolated mountain region – outdoor recreation. The pack business in Mammoth Lakes has grown right along with it.

Today, one of the most successful pack stations in the Eastern Sierra is also the oldest – Mammoth Lakes Pack Outfit. Located on the site of Pine City, an old mining camp between Twin Lake and Lake Mary, it has been owned since 1960 by Lou and Mary Roeser.

As one of the larger operations in the Sierra Nevada, Mammoth Lakes offers everything from one-hour rides in the immediate vicinity to extended trips into the John Muir Wilderness.

The one-hour trip, offered at 9:30 a.m., 11:00 a.m., 2:00 p.m. and 3:45 p.m., is a simple ride through a forest of red fir and then up about a third of the way to the top of Red Mountain. Once the site of a brief mining boom back in the late 1870s, it provides an excellent view of Mammoth Crest behind it and the Mammoth Lakes basin below.

For even better views, riders might consider the two-hour trip to Heart Lake, departing every morning at 8:30 a.m. Proceeding along a trail that goes past Cold Water Campground, riders enter an area near Mammoth Creek that is filled with wildflowers. Farther up, they catch panoramic views of Mammoth Crescent, Mammoth Mountain, and the Ritter Range off beyond Mammoth Pass.

Eventually, they reach Heart Lake, sitting on the slope of Red Mountain at 9,590 feet elevation, and the inspiration for its name becomes clear. The shore of the lake curves around in the perfect shape of a heart. After enjoying the scenery, riders head back down.

Mammoth Lakes Pack Outfit offers an alternative two-hour ride at 1:15 p.m. that goes up to Barret Lake and then over a small ridge to T.J. Lake. During the trip, riders are treated to a colorful display of wildflowers along the shore of T.J. Lake and scenic views of the nearby mountains.

Each week on Monday and Thursday, there is a half-day ride to Arrowhead Lake and Skelton Lake that departs at 8:00 a.m. Basically, this follows the same trail through Cold Water Campground that is used for the Heart Lake trip. But, instead of cutting over to Heart Lake, riders continue up Cold Water Canyon, following the course of Mammoth Creek through a forest of lodgepole pine. At 9,660 feet elevation, riders reach Arrowhead Lake, peeking out from behind the trees.

It is only a half mile more to Skelton Lake, once the site of a stamp mill. At this point, riders have an opportunity to get off their horses and enjoy the scenery, before returning to the pack station.

On Tuesday, there is an alternative half-day ride that goes right up to the Mammoth Crest. Following a trail that goes past Lake George and Crystal Lake, riders climb up into an area behind the Crystal Crag. A relatively flat area is reached, where riders can dismount and take in the sights. From the Mammoth Crest, they have a breathtaking panoramic view of the Ritter Range to the west and out across the lakes basin to the east. After remounting their horses, they work their way back down to the pack station.

Riders looking for a true wilderness experience without having to camp overnight might consider the all-day trip, scheduled every Wednesday. Following the same trail that goes to Arrowhead Lake and Skelton Lake, riders continue up through mountain meadows, past greenish-colored Barney Lake, and over 10,790 foot high Duck Pass.

At the pass, above the tree line, there is loose shale on both sides of the rocky trail. But even in this barren, alpine terrain, occasional wildflowers poke out, providing unexpected bursts of color. Soon, Duck Lake comes into view. What catches the eye first is its rich, blue color, uncommon in the Sierra. Set against the rugged high mountain scenery, the blue is quite striking. Near the lake, there are few trees, but a meadow extends part way around.

Riders stop at Duck Lake for several hours to eat lunch, fish, relax, and, of course, take pictures. Then they return over the pass and follow the trail back down.

Pack Trips

There is also the opportunity to travel over the Duck Pass on several of the all-inclusive pack trips that Mammoth Lakes Pack Outfit offers each year. Early in the season, riders can take a five-day trip that goes up over the pass, down past scenic Purple Lake to Fish Creek in the Cascade Valley. At that time of year, there is still plenty of water in the waterfalls in the area and the fishing in the lakes and streams is excellent.

Later in the season, the pack outfit returns to this area on a four-day trip. But instead of camping down in the Cascade Valley, the group stops at Purple Lake, and makes a day trip to Fish Creek. The longer stay at Purple Lake gives riders a chance to enjoy its rare beauty. In a picture-postcard setting, trees dot the slope above the lake and a lush green meadow comes right up to its shore. Nearby, wildflowers line the edge of rock-filled Purple Creek.

As an alternative, riders can take a four-day trip with overnight stays at Purple Lake and a day trip to Virginia Lake, a popular fishing spot promising great golden trout.

The premier trip in this area, however, is the six-day journey down to McGee Creek. From Mammoth, riders head up over Duck Pass, and then down past Purple Lake and Virgina Lake to Tully Hole, a lush, green meadow. From Tully Hole, they swing around along a trail that follows upper Fish Creek and goes up over 12,000 foot high McGee Pass. Following the trail down through McGee Creek Canyon, they end the trip at the McGee Creek trailhead, passing magnificent Horsetail Falls along the way.

Another outstanding six-day trip goes into the Silver Divide area, considered the most scenic in the John Muir Wilderness. Base camp is established at Grassy Lake, a delightful alpine setting for fishing, hiking, and relaxing.

Special Programs

Mammoth Lakes Pack Outfit also offers several special programs. Fishing enthusiasts might consider the five-day wilderness fly-fishing class. Artists can try their hand at painting in the wilderness with a trained instructor as part of the week-long watercolor program. In addition, riders can learn more about horsemanship and packing in a special instructional program.

During the wintertime, Mammoth Lakes Pack Outfit is closed. However, nearby Sierra Meadows Equestrian Center, also owned by the Roesers, is open year round. On weekends and holidays, riders can take one-hour trips through the snow-covered meadows or up around Mammoth Creek. Sleigh rides are also available.

Horse Drives

Among the best known and most popular horse drives in the Eastern Sierra are those conducted by Mammoth Lakes Pack Outfit. Riders come back year after year as they pursue the silver belt buckle that signifies membership in the exclusive "Thousand Mile Club," an honor reserved for those who have completed ten drives.

They also come back for the great riding, good fellowship, and the thrill of discovering they are capable of doing things they didn't realize they could do. For anyone who loves to ride horses, it doesn't get much better than this.

Beginning in the middle of June each year, the Roeser family, the pack station staff, and 50 guests head out from the winter pasture land in the Owens Valley with 130 head of horses and mules. Following a route that has become fairly standard for most packers in the region, they head up the Sherwin grade into the national forest north of Bishop. From there, they continue around past Crowley Lake, and over to Sierra Meadows Equestrian Center in Mammoth.

Because the drives have become so popular, the Roesers now conduct the spring drive twice, allowing more people to participate.

During the drives, they make overnight stops at Casa Diablo Mountain Camp, Layton Springs Camp, Arcularius Ranch Camp, and Long Valley Camp. Evenings are spent reading cowboy poetry, performing skits, and listening to the good-time tunes of traveling musicians Fiddlin' Pete and Derik.

For those who hate to see it end, they always know that in October, the horses have to come back down to the Owens Valley again.

Rates

The one-hour ride is $25 and the two-hour ride is $35. The half-day ride is $45 and the all-day ride is $70. The five-day trip to Cascade Valley is $650. The four-day trip to Cascade Valley is $520. The four-day trips to Virginia Lake and to Purple Lake are $520 each. The six-day trip to McGee Creek is $800 and the six-day trip to Grassy Lake is $650.

The fly-fishing trip is $650 and the six-day watercolor workshop in the wilderness is $725. Write the pack station for the professional packing and horsemanship school rates.

Spot trips range in price from $225 to $570 per person for a party of two, depending upon the destination. Extended trips are $110 per day for the packer, $55 per day per animal for pack mules and saddle horses.

All-inclusive trips are $160 per person per day for parties from four to nine, and $150 per person per day for parties of ten or more. The first spring horse drive is $650. The second spring drive is $725. The two fall horse drives are $650 each.

One-hour trail rides in the winter are $25 and sleigh rides are $25 for adults, $20 for children under 12, and $15 for children under six.

Payment Method

Mammoth Lakes Pack Outfit accepts cash, personal checks, traveler's checks, Visa, and MasterCard.

Rider Age Limit

For the one-hour trip, riders must be at least seven years old. For all other trips, they must be at least eight years old.

How To Get There

From Highway 395, take the Mammoth Lakes turn off. Follow Highway 203 into Mammoth Lakes. At the post office, turn left on Lake Mary Road. Proceed on Lake Mary Road to a point between Lake Mary and Twin Lakes. The pack station is on the right.

RED'S MEADOW PACK STATION

P.O. Box 395
Mammoth Lakes, CA 93546
(619) 934-2345 (Summer)
(619) 873-3928 (Winter)
Owner: Bob Tanner

For 15 years, from 1890 to 1905, Devil's Postpile and more than 500 square miles of adjacent lands, including the Minarets and breathtaking Rainbow Falls, were part of Yosemite National Park. That they are not still included in the park speaks volumes about the political power that mining and lumbering interests once possessed.

Fortunately, through the diligent efforts of concerned citizens, the area has ultimately been saved. Today, Devil's Postpile and Rainbow Falls are part of a national monument, and the rest of the land is protected by the U.S. Forest Service. It's a beautiful area, well worth exploring, and for trail riders there's a practical way to explore it.

Red's Meadow Pack Station, located at the western base of Mammoth Mountain, offers trail rides through the surrounding 500 square miles and well inside Yosemite itself from mid-June through late September.

The shortest of these is the two-hour ride down to Rainbow Falls and back. Leaving from the pack station at 8:30 a.m., 11:00 a.m., and 2:00 p.m., riders proceed down a trail that winds through a forest of lodgepole pine, white fir and red fir. The trail itself is made of finely-ground pumice, clear evidence of the volcanic activity in the area. This is no surprise, of course, Rainbow Falls is only a few miles downstream from one of nature's most famous volcanic phenomena, Devil's Postpile.

Upon arrival at the falls, riders dismount and tie up their horses at the hitching post. They then take several minutes to enjoy the waterfall that well-know mountaineer Walter Starr, Jr. once described as "the most beautiful in the Sierra outside of Yosemite." Few would disagree. From a rugged volcanic ledge, a huge wall of water tumbles 101 feet down and crashes on the rocks below, sending up a mist that catches the sun in a brilliant rainbow of color.

For the best photographs of the rainbow effect, riders should choose the 11:00 a.m. trip. It arrives at the falls just when the sun is in the right position. After remounting, riders continue down to Lower Falls, before returning back up through the woods to the pack station.

On the half-day trips, which depart at 8:00 a.m. and 1:00 p.m., riders follow the John Muir Trail over to the Red Cones and climb up to the top of the North Cone. From the barren, cratered top, riders have a panoramic view in several directions. Off to one side is the imposing Ritter Range. Off to another is San Joaquin Ridge. Swinging around, riders can look out over the John Muir Wilderness.

Rainbow fall's near Devil's Postpile

Continuing down the other side, they pass through Crater Meadows, resplendent with wildflowers in the summer, and then loop around to the Mammoth Pass Trail for the return to the pack station. Riders generally spend about three hours in the saddle on the half-day trip.

The all-day trips leave from Agnew Meadow Pack Station, also owned by Bob Tanner and located just a few miles up the Minaret Summit road. Riders have a choice of going to Clark Lakes, Thousand Island Lake, or Ediza Lake for an hour or two of fishing and sightseeing.

Pack Trips

For riders looking for an extended vacation in the wilderness, Red's Meadow Pack Station offers a number of all-inclusive trips.

Early in the summer and then again late in the summer, the pack station schedules a six-day trip into the Fish Creek Valley region of the John Muir Wilderness. Riders follow a trail that goes down along Crater Creek, and then over to Island Crossing, Iva Belle Camp, and Cascade Valley. During the six days, side trips are taken to Beetlebug Lake, Minnow Creek, Lake of the Lone Indian, and upper Fish Creek. Riders return by way of Purple Lake along the John Muir Trail.

Red's Meadow Pack Station also offers several five-day trips into some of the same areas serviced by Frontier Pack Train. Riders depart from Agnew Meadow Pack Station and travel up to Thousand Island Lake along the exceptionally scenic High Trail. Along the way, they are treated to awesome views of the craggy, glacier-spotted Ritter Range, while crossing numerous mountain streams brightly lined with wildflowers.

Riders lay over at Thousand Island Lake, before continuing along the John Muir Trail to Shadow Creek below Lake Ediza. A second camp is established here. Riders then return along the John Muir Trail to Red's Meadow, passing near Devil's Postpile along the way.

Several trips into Yosemite National Park are offered each year, as well. The six-day trip to Tuolumne Meadows that starts from Agnew Meadow is similar in many respects to the Frontier Pack Train trip previously described. However, Red's Meadow Pack Station has two other trips that are a good deal more ambitious.

The eight-day trip into Yosemite begins like the six-day trip. Riders travel over the Donohue Pass, but then at Kuna Creek, rather than continuing to Tuolumne Meadows, they head down to Vogelsang. From Vogelsang, they travel to Merced Lake, and then on to Little Yosemite Valley. Swinging around, they go past Half Dome and up to Clouds Rest. From Clouds Rest, they follow the Sunrise Trail up through Cathedral Meadows to Tuolumne Meadows. Transportation is then provided back to the pack station.

Red's Meadow Pack Station also offers six-day trips along the John Muir Trail to McGee Creek that are quite similar to those offered by Mammoth Lakes Pack Station. They also schedule a seven-day trip to Rock Creek that follows a trail over Silver Pass and Mono Pass, providing riders with outstanding views of the beautiful high Sierra countryside. Overnight stops on this trip are at Mono Creek and Fish Creek.

Special Programs

In addition, Red's Meadow Pack Station schedules special trips for photographers, fly fishermen, and parents traveling with children.

There is also a back country cooking trip, where riders can learn the art of cooking on the trail. For riders interested in learning more about the art of packing, the pack station offers a packing school. The seven-day program provides professional instruction in horsemanship and packing skills.

Horse Drives

Like many of the pack stations in the Eastern Sierra, Red's Meadow conducts a horse drive at the beginning and the end of each season. It's an opportunity for 30 individuals to do the kind of wide-open riding that is rarely possible on the typical trail ride. For the most part, the Red's Meadow Pack Station horse drives closely follow the route established by Mammoth Lakes Pack Station. The fall drive even begins at Sierra Meadows Equestrian Center in Mammoth.

The drives, which last three days, stop one night above Crowley Lake and the other night at Casa Diablo. The Rocking K Ranch in Bishop serves as the starting point for the spring drive and as the final stop for the fall drive. As with all horse drives, it's important to reserve early, because they are extremely popular.

Rates

The two-hour ride is $25. The half-day ride is $40 and the all-day ride is $60. The six-day trip to Fish Creek and the five-day trip to Thousand Island Lake are $595 each. The six-day trip to Tuolumne Meadows is $650. The six-day trip to McGee Creek is $645 and the seven-day trip to Rock Creek is $695.

The five-day photography trip is $595 and the six-day fly-fishing trip is $595. The five-day trip for parents and children is $550 for adults and $350 for children. The four-day back country cooking trip is $450 and the seven-day packing school is $650. The three-day horse drives are $450.

Spot trips are $275 for parties of four or more. Parties of three are $285 and parties of two are $330. Custom all-inclusive trips are $160 per day for parties of five or more. Parties of four are $170 per day and parties of three are $190 per day.

Payment Method

Red's Meadow Pack Station accepts cash, personal checks, and traveler's checks.

Rider Age Limit

Riders must be at least six years old. Younger children may double with a parent, at no extra charge.

How To Get There

From Highway 395, 40 miles north of Bishop, take the Highway 203 turn off. Follow the road through Mammoth Lakes and up to the Mammoth Ski Area. Continue past the ski area over Minaret Summit to the U.S. Forest Service office. Show your pack trip reservation and you will be permitted to continue. Agnew Meadow is two miles and Red's Meadow is eight miles from Minaret Summit. Vacationers without reservations, must take the shuttle bus from the ski area parking lot to either Agnew Meadow and Red's Meadow.

MCGEE CREEK PACK STATION

Rt. 1, Box 162
Mammoth Lakes, California 93546
(619) 935-4324 (Summer)
(619) 878-2207 (Winter)
Owners: Lee and Jennifer Roeser

It's easy for motorists to miss McGee Creek Canyon as they race up Highway 395 on their way to Mammoth. Except for a single road sign identifying the turn off, there is little to indicate all that lies up beyond the rolling hills of sagebrush visible from the highway.

That's unfortunate, however, because if motorists were to venture just a short distance up McGee Creek Road, they would discover a ruggedly beautiful canyon, the sculpted handiwork of an ancient glacier. Continuing further, they would hear the soothing gurgles of McGee Creek, and they would catch the splendid sight of Horsetail Falls cascading majestically down the sheer rock face at the end of the canyon. Once they'd had a good look, they'd be motivated to explore more.

Fortunately, there's a convenient and enjoyable way to continue exploring. McGee Creek Pack Station, owned and operated by Lee and Jennifer Roeser, offers trips from mid-June to early October that go throughout the canyon and beyond.

The easiest of these are the one- and two-hour rides. On the one-hour trip, riders follow a simple loop trail that goes up into the canyon for a ways before swinging around and returning to the pack station along McGee Creek.

On the two-hour trip, riders head off in a similar direction, but instead of turning around at the same spot, they continue on to Horsetail Falls. Along the way, they view the interesting rock formations and multi-colored canyon walls, which reveal many clues about the region's geologic history. After enjoying the falls up close and snapping some photos, riders turn around and head back.

The view up McGee Canyon from McGee Creek Pack Station

Twice daily, at 8 a.m. and 1:00 p.m., riders leave on a half-day trip to Beaver Meadow. Upon arriving at the beautiful mountain meadow on McGee Creek, they get off their horses to enjoy the scenery and eat a snack. After a half-hour stop, they return to the pack station.

For a longer ride that focuses on fishing, vacationers might consider one of the three all-day trips. The first goes up to Round Lake. For this trip, riders follow McGee Creek upstream through the canyon along a trail that is unshaded for several miles, before entering a forest of lodgepole pine. After a steep climb up to 9,950 feet in elevation, they reach Round Lake.

Once at the lake, riders break out the fishing tackle, which is carried up on an extra pack animal provided for the trip. Several hours are set aside for fishing, eating lunch, and relaxing. The second trip is quite similar. It even follows the same trail for the first several miles, before veering off to the east. On this trip, riders go up to Grass Lake, sitting at 9,800 feet in elevation, amidst a beautiful meadow, which also offers excellent fishing.

The third option to Hilton Lakes leaves in a somewhat different direction. Riders must head east around the mountain to get to the lakes, a journey requiring between three and three and a half hours. Because of the longer ride, there is less time for fishing on this trip.

Pack Trips

There are also longer trips available that will satisfy fishermen and non-fishermen alike. The most popular of these are the "Wilderness Discovery Rides," all-inclusive six-day trips that go from McGee Creek to Mammoth Lakes. During these journeys through the John Muir Wilderness, riders encounter remarkable changes in scenery, terrain, geology, and plant life.

On the first day of the trip, riders head up along the trail used for the trip to Round Lake. But, instead of stopping there, they continue on to Big McGee Lake, which sits in the shadow of Mount Crocker and Red and White Mountain at 10,480 feet in elevation. Camp is established there for the first night.

The following day, riders make the steep climb up McGee Pass at 11,900 feet. After crossing the pass, the route can vary depending upon the interests of the group. Riders can go either to Horse Heaven and Tully Hole or to upper Fish Creek. At either location, the group will layover for a day. The Tully Hole layover will provide the chance for stream fishing and the upper Fish Creek layover will allow for lake fishing.

Three options exist for the fourth day of the trip. Riders can either go to Grassy Lake in the Silver Divide area, to Cascade Valley, or to Purple Lake by way of Lake Virginia. There is a layover on the fifth day and on the sixth day, they ride out to Mammoth Lakes.

The "Wilderness Discovery Rides" can also be taken in the reverse direction, departing from Mammoth Lakes and ending up in McGee Creek.

Horse Drives

McGee Creek Pack Station is linked quite closely with Mammoth Lakes Pack Station. Lee and Jennifer Roeser are the son and daughter-in-law of Lou and Mary Roeser, owners of the Mammoth Lakes operation. During the fall and spring horse drives, the two pack stations join forces, with Lou and Lee acting as the leaders. For more information, turn to the section on Mammoth Lakes Pack Station.

Rates

The one-hour ride is $20 and the two-hour ride is $25. The half-day rides are $35 and the all-day rides are $50. The Wilderness Discovery Rides are $800. Extended trips are $95 per day for the packer with horse and $45 per day for each additional pack animal. One-day spot trips are $295 for two people, $265 for three or four people, $240 for five to nine people, and $225 for ten or more people. The two-day spot trips are $440 for two people, $390 for three to four people, $365 for five to nine people, and $340 for ten or more people.

Payment Method

McGee Creek Pack Station accepts cash, personal checks, traveler's checks, and American Express.

Rider Age Limit

Riders must be at least six years old.

How To Get There

From Highway 395, ten miles south of Mammoth Lakes and 30 miles north of Bishop, turn off on McGee Creek Road. Proceed for three miles and look for the pack station on the left.

PINE CREEK PACK TRAINS

P.O. Box 968
Bishop, CA 93515
(619) 387-2797
Owners: Brian and Danica Berner

There was a time late in the 19th century when mining activity flourished throughout the Eastern Sierra. It didn't last long, of course. In many areas, the transition from boom town to ghost town happened almost overnight.

Unlike in neighboring canyons, the Pine Creek mining activity was later resumed – thanks to a strong demand for tungsten – and it continues today. Continuing right along with it has been Pine Creek Pack Trains, originally started to carry men and supplies to the mine.

These days, the pack station helps vacationers discover a treasure that's even more valuable and rare – the unmatched beauty of the Sierra Nevada.

Each year from June 1 through September 30, Pine Creek Pack Trains organizes trips in and around the nearby canyons and off into John Muir Wilderness.

The easiest of these, the day trip, goes to one of three locations. Riders can follow Pine Creek up to Pine Lake – roughly a two-and-a-half-hour ride – or they can take the same trail farther up to Honeymoon Lake. A third choice is to head up through Morgan Canyon to Lower Morgan Lake. Of the three options, the ride to Pine Lake involves the least amount of time in the saddle and allows the most time for fishing. The other two trips are at least an hour longer, leaving plenty of time for a leisurely lunch, but less for fishing.

Pine Creek Pack Station

Pack Trips

Pine Creek Pack Trains' all-inclusive trips frequently follow these same scenic trails. There are four and five day trips that visit prime fishing spots like Hilton Lakes, Morgan Lakes, and Upper Pine Lake.

Maybe the best trip for fishermen, however, is the five-day trip into French Canyon, an area in the John Muir Wilderness known for trophy-size golden trout. To reach the canyon, riders follow a trail that goes up past Pine Lake and over 11,120 foot high Pine Creek Pass, stopping for the first night at French Creek. During their travels riders stop in the Hutchinson Meadows area for stream fishing and then continue on to Humphreys Basin for lake fishing. Normally, they set up camp either at Packsaddle Lake or Piute Creek. On the final day, they return to the pack station over Pine Creek Pass.

A somewhat more ambitious six-day trip starts along the same trail through Pine Creek Pass. Time is spent in the French Canyon area, before riders continue down to the John Muir Trail. Near the trail junction, riders cross a steel bridge into Kings Canyon National Park and proceed down into Evolution Valley, crossing many streams along the way. The group makes an overnight stop at Evolution Meadows, a lunch stop at McClure Meadows, and another overnight stop at Colby Meadow.

The trail then takes them past Evolution Lake, Wanda Lake, up over rocky, desolate Muir Pass, and down into Le Conte Canyon. The last stop along the way is at Big Pete Meadow. Riders then depart from Kings Canyon National Park over 11,972 foot high Bishop Pass and complete their trip at South Lake. Transportation is provided from there back to Pine Creek.

The highlight for photographers, however, has to be the "Fall Colors Photography Ride." On the two-day trip, riders head over to Hilton Creek, traveling through forests of aspen, birch, alder, willow, and cottonwood and through meadows of wild grasses grown tall during the summer. Along the way, there are numerous opportunities to capture on film the fall foliage in all its many-colored splendor. It's a fitting way to mark the end of the Sierra summer season.

Horse Drive

The four-day horse drive offered by Pine Creek Pack Trains is somewhat different than other horse drives. It's offered only in the fall and usually involves no more than 80 horses. In addition, only ten guests are invited to participate. This, of course, makes for a more intimate experience.

Beginning at Crowley Lake, riders travel south to Lone Pine, with overnight stops at Mill Pond Campgrounds, Baker Creek Campgrounds, and Tinemaha.

Rates

The all-day ride is $60. Lunch is available for an additional six dollars. Write to the pack station for other rates.

Payment Method

Pine Creek Pack Station accepts cash, personal checks, and traveler's checks.

Rider Age Limit

Riders must be at least six years old.

How To Get There

From Highway 395, ten miles north of Bishop, take the Pine Creek exit. Go nine miles down the road to the pack station.

ROCK CREEK PACK STATION

P.O. Box 248
Bishop, CA 93515
(619) 935-4493 (Summer)
(619) 872-8331 (Winter)
Owners: Craig London, Herb London and Dave Dohnel

There are many points in the Eastern Sierra higher in elevation than Rock Creek Canyon. Not the least of which is Mount Whitney, highest spot in the contiguous 48 states. But there is no other motor thoroughfare in the region that goes as high as modern, paved Rock Creek Road. At Mosquito Flat, where it ends, the road reaches 10,200 feet in elevation, higher even than Tioga Pass. From that elevation, the Sierra high country becomes unusually accessible.

Little wonder then that one of the largest pack outfits in all of the Sierra is located nearby. Rock Creek Pack Station, which has government permits to operate from Lake Tahoe to Lake Isabella, arranges trips of various lengths that go all over the Sierra Nevada.

With so many big trips to organize and run each year, however, the pack station tends to not emphasize half-day and day rides. They offer them. But, they are subject to the availability of horses, and clearly the longer trips have priority.

Vacationers looking for a short ride on a horse, might be better served at one of the other pack stations. If they're looking for a longer ride, however, they'll find plenty to choose from. Some of the trips are primarily intended for the different educational institutions, including UCLA, that have contracts with the pack station. But many more are open to anyone who is interested.

Pack Trips

The shortest and easiest all-inclusive trip is the four-day trip over to Mono Creek. Beginning at the pack station, a short distance above Rock Creek Lake, riders proceed to Little Lakes Valley, a beautiful open, flat area covered with wild grasses, dotted with wildflowers, and surrounded by magnificent mountain peaks. They then climb a series of switchbacks over Mono Pass, catching a great view along the way of 13,748 foot high Mount Morgan rising above Little Lakes Valley.

They continue down into the Mono Creek area, where camp is established. During their stay, riders take excursions to Pioneer Basin,

Hopkins Basin, and Fourth Recess Lake to fish for golden trout or simply to relax. On the final day, they return to Rock Creek.

A five-day trip from Rock Creek to Mammoth Lakes also passes through Little Lakes Valley, over Mono Pass, and into the Mono Creek area. But then it continues on over Silver Pass and down into the scenic Cascade Valley. Side trips are taken to Jackson Meadow and Grassy Lake or over to the hot springs near Iva Belle Camp. From Cascade Valley, riders follow the trail up past Purple Lake, Duck Lake, and over Duck Pass. The trip ends at Lake Mary.

For a slight variation, riders can take a seven-day trip to Red's Meadow. The trip begins along the same route as the Mammoth Lakes trip. However, after crossing Silver Pass, riders camp either at Grassy Lake or Wilbur May Lake. On a layover day, they explore the nearby Minnow Creek area. Continuing on to Fish Creek, riders stop off to visit the hot springs near Iva Belle Camp. From Fish Creek, they follow a trail along Crater Creek up past Red Cones to Red's Meadow.

Adventurous riders, prepared to go a long distance in the saddle, might consider the 12-day Rock Creek to Bishop Creek trip. It's a rare opportunity to travel along a long portion of the John Muir Trail through the magnificent high country of Kings Canyon National Park.

Beginning their wilderness expedition with a pleasant ride up through Little Lakes Valley, riders head over 12,000 foot high Mono Pass into the Mono Creek area. Then, following the creek west, they meet up with the John Muir Trail and follow it down through the forest into the Bear Creek area. Continuing on, riders pass through Rosemarie Meadow and skirt Marie Lake before going over 10,900 foot Selden Pass. Looking back down from the pass, riders have a splendid view of island-dotted Marie Lake.

Some distance down the trail, riders cross the steel bridge into Kings Canyon National Park and then continue on to Evolution Valley. The trail takes them through McClure Meadow, Colby Meadow, and past Evolution Lake. Traveling through a barren, glacier-sculpted alpine landscape, riders continue on past Sapphire Lake and Wanda Lake, before crossing rocky, desolate Muir Pass.

The terrain remains treeless as riders pass Helen Lake, a few hundred feet below the summit. Eventually, they drop below the treeline as they travel through LeConte Canyon. On the final leg of the trip, riders go up over Bishop Pass and down to the trailhead at South Lake.

Rock Creek Pack Station's other long-distance expedition is probably their premier ride, a 12-day trip to Tuolumne Meadows. It is not the only trip of its kind offered, of course. Both Frontier Pack Train and Red's Meadow Pack Station offer similar trips, but this one covers more territory. For those who have the time, it's an opportunity to enjoy a number of the Sierra's most spectacular highlights.

During the 12 days, riders travel over Mono Pass, through the Mono Creek area, and up over Silver Pass. They head down into the Cascade Valley, along Fish Creek, and up through the Ansel Adams Wilderness. They catch panoramic views of Mt. Ritter, Banner Peak, and the Minarets as they continue past Thousand Island Lake and up over Donohue Pass. They make one last stop at Kuna Creek and Lyell Fork, for an excursion to Vogelsang, before riding out to Tuolumne Meadows on the 12th day. Transportation is provided back to the pack station.

Wild Mustang Observation

Rock Creek Pack Station is one of two outfits in the eastern Sierra that offer special trips into the Pizona area of the Inyo National Forest, where several hundred mustangs run wild and free. During the four-day trip, riders have a chance to observe and photograph the horses up close and to learn more about their history and behavior.

The first morning of the trip, riders are transported from Bishop out to River Springs, where they receive their horses. Then the group rides out to the camp at Pizona Springs. The next two days are spent tracking and viewing the horses across the open range. Throughout the four days, seminars are provided on the history, social structure, and behavior of the horses. There is even a discussion about how individuals may obtain, train, and use a wild horse.

On the final afternoon, riders are transported back to Bishop.

Horse Drives

The highlights of the year for many riders may be the spring and fall horse drives that begin and end the season. They offer riders the chance to use skills they normally don't get to test and they do so in an environment of fellowship and good cheer. Typically, 20 to 25 guests are invited along to help drive between 100 and 120 head of horses and mules.

The spring drive begins out on 6,000 acres east of Independence, where the horses and mules spend their winter months grazing. The group begins moving north through the open pastures, before crossing over Highway 395 at a spot between Big Pine and Bishop.

The drive stops for the night above Big Pine at Baker Creek. The following day, the group pushes on to Mill Pond, where they stop for the second night. Pushing on towards the mountains, the group makes it to Swall Meadows at the base of Sand Canyon for their last night under the stars. The following day, they bring the herd up to the pack station near Rock Creek Lake.

The fall drive goes back down to Independence along essentially the same route.

Cattle Drives

Rock Creek Pack Station does not offer a regularly scheduled cattle drive. However, they do run cattle drives from time to time and guests are invited along. It requires some flexibility, though, because word about a cattle drive generally comes with rather short notice.

Those interested in being called about a drive, must place their names on a waiting list. It's certainly not the ideal arrangement. But given the enormous popularity of cattle drives, and the small number of drives available, this kind of stand-by approach may be the only way for some people to have a chance to participate.

Rates

Half-day rides are $35 and all-day rides are $55. The four-day trip to Mono Creek is $420. The five-day trip to Mammoth Lakes is $550. The seven-day trip to Red's Meadow is $725. The 12-day trip to Bishop Pass is $1120 and the 12-day trip to Tuolumne Meadows is $1225. The wild mustang trip is $425 and the horse drives are $550. Extended trips are $110 per day for packer with horse and $50 per day for each additional pack animal. Spot trips range in price from $195 to $470 depending upon the destination and the number in the party.

Payment Method

Rock Creek Pack Station accepts cash, personal checks, and traveler's checks.

Rider Age Limit

Riders must be at least six years old, with no exceptions.

How To Get There

From Highway 395, 24 miles north of Bishop, take the Rock Creek Lake exit. Proceed along the road approximately eight miles and look for the pack station sign on the right.

COTTONWOOD PACK STATION

Star Route Box 81-A
Independence, CA 93526
(619) 878-2015
Owners: Dennis and Jody Winchester

All too often when people try to get away from it all these days, they discover that a large number of their fellow citizens have decided to get away from it all along with them.

One place they might consider in seeking refuge from the crowds is the southern end of the Eastern Sierra, an area that receives fewer visitors than elsewhere in the 400-mile long range. Partly, this is due to the terrain. The mountains in the southeast are more rounded, lacking the dramatic jagged countenance of their northerly neighbors. This aside, however, the region abounds with visual delights all its own. In addition, the fishing in its lakes and streams is excellent. Best of all for trail riders, it's easily accessible by horse.

From mid-June through late September each year, Cottonwood Pack Station, located in the Horseshoe Meadow area of the Golden Trout Wilderness, offers all-inclusive pack trips that visit the most scenic portions of the southeastern Sierra.

The most convenient of these for people with busy schedules is the three-day weekend trip to Big Whitney Meadow. Leaving from Horseshoe Meadow bright and early Friday morning, riders begin a climb that takes them up over 11,200 foot high Cottonwood Pass. They then work their way down through a series of switchbacks to Big Whitney Meadow, 1,400 feet below.

The first order of business, when they arrive at camp, is to eat lunch. After that, some riders stay around the camp and relax, while others head off for an afternoon ride to either Rocky Basin Lakes or Johnson Lake for fishing, hiking, or picture taking.

The following morning, campers have the option of going for another day ride or staying around camp to enjoy the fresh air, alpine vistas, and nearby mountain stream. On Sunday morning, campers begin the ride out, making a side trip to Chicken Spring Lake along the way. They arrive back at the pack station well before dinner.

Riders with more time available have the opportunity to go up into Sequoia National Park on the four-day trip. Their journey begins along the same route as the three-day trip, up over Cottonwood Pass. But instead of going down to Big Whitney Meadow, they swing onto the Pacific Crest Trail, which passes Chicken Spring Lake. Continuing on towards the national park, riders have an excellent view of the wide, green expanse of Big Whitney Meadow far below. Looking ahead, they take in a sweeping panorama of the snow-patched Great Western Divide.

After entering the national park, they drop down below the timberline into a thick pine forest. Near Rock Creek, riders head off on a trail that follows the stream up into the Miter Basin. Base camp for the trip is established here in the shadow of the southernmost peaks in the Sierra Nevada to exceed 13,000 feet.

During their stay, riders fish for golden trout in Rock Creek, and in some of the nearby lakes, including Sky-Blue Lake. On the third day, the group ventures down to the grassy meadows around lower Rock Creek for more fishing. Mount Whitney, visible during this excursion, provides riders with a great photo opportunity.

On the final day, they ride up out of the park and stop for a final round of fishing at Chicken Spring Lake. Then it's up over the pass and back to the pack station.

For a more extensive exploration of the Golden Trout Wilderness, riders might consider the five-day trip. It begins with the group traveling up over Trail Pass and down into Mulkey Meadows. They continue on to Golden Trout Creek, near the South Fork Kern River, where camp is established for the first night.

On the second day, riders linger around camp or fish in the nearby streams, before riding on to Little Whitney Meadow for the night. The third day is the most scenic and interesting of the trip. Riders travel down a trail that goes through a lava field, over the Natural Bridge, and past Volcano Falls. They stop alongside the Kern River for lunch. After lunch, riders have a choice of either spending time fishing or visiting nearby Soda Springs. They then return to Little Whitney Meadow for a second night.

The following morning, the group rides up to Big Whitney Meadow, where camp is established in the pine forest at the meadow's edge. A group then rides over to Rocky Basin Lakes for an afternoon of fishing, while the rest of the riders kick back and relax in camp.

On the final day, riders make the climb up to Cottonwood Pass and then swing over to Chicken Spring Lake. After a few more hours of fishing, they travel back down to the pack station.

Rates

The three-day all-inclusive trip is $350, the four-day trip is $500, and the five-day is $500. Extended trips are $90 per day for a packer with horse and $50 per day for each additional horse or mule. One-day spot trips are $290 per person for parties of two, $260 per person for parties of three, $245 per person for parties of four, and $236 per person for parties of five. Two-day spot trips range in price from $354 to $580, depending upon the destination and the number in the party.

Payment Method

Cottonwood Pack Station accepts cash, personal checks, and traveler's checks

Rider Age Limit

There is no specific age limit. However, depending upon their size and riding ability, younger children may be required to double up with a parent.

How To Get There

From Highway 395 at Lone Pine, take Whitney Portal Road west for five miles. Turn off onto Horseshoe Meadow Road. Go approximately 20 miles to the pack station.

FURNACE CREEK STABLES

P.O. Box 418
Death Valley, CA 92328
(619) 786-2345, Ext. 230
Owner: Mark Berry

It's hard to imagine a place anywhere in the United States more desolate or more forbidding than Death Valley in the eastern Mojave Desert of California.

As the seasons change and the scorching heat of summer begins to moderate, this rugged valley, much of it below sea level, becomes an interesting and enjoyable place to visit. Automobiles, of course, provide the most effective means of touring the 3,231 square miles within Death Valley National Monument. But when you reach Furnace Creek, it's time to get out from behind the wheel and up into the saddle.

Furnace Creek Stables, open from October 1 through May 1 each year, offers one-, two-, and three-hour trail rides in and around the Furnace Creek area. Leading the trips are veteran wranglers from respected McGee Creek Pack Station who spend their winters at Death Valley.

On the one-hour trip, riders head out from the stables, located not far from the Borax Museum, past the Furnace Creek Ranch Golf Course into the wide-open floor of the valley. Following a simple loop route, riders travel through a desert landscape that contains little more than occasional mesquite trees and long, barren salt flats.

Looking off to the west, they have a sweeping view of the rugged Panamint Mountains. Back in 1849, this range of mountains had seemed all but impenetrable to the Bennett-Arcane Party, the first non-Native American visitors to the valley. It was their almost month-long struggle to find a way past the mountains, with food and water running low, that earned the desert valley its name. As they finally made their escape, one member of the group exclaimed, "Goodbye, Death Valley."

During winter months, the Panamint Mountains are particularly scenic, because they are frequently covered with snow. As riders continue their loop through the salt flats, they also have an excellent view of the Funeral Mountains, that run along the California-Nevada border.

Packing demonstration at Furnace Creek Ranch

On the two-hour trip, riders travel up into the foothills of the Funeral Mountains behind the Furnace Creek Inn. Leaving from the stables, sitting at 180 feet below sea level, they climb past the Inn, which sits right at sea level. Originally constructed in 1926 by the Pacific Coast Borax Company for its employees, the Furnace Creek Inn, today, provides the most luxurious guest accommodations available in Death Valley National Monument.

Continuing, they ride through the barren, cream-colored foothills, shaped by infrequent, but rather violent rain storms and by the often-present wind. Winding through the foothills, they swing through Indian Springs and Texas Springs, site of a park campground. Along the way, riders catch outstanding views of the valley stretching out below and of the formidable Panamint Range beyond. Occasionally, they spot coyotes and bobcats along the trail and frequently a hawk can be seen quietly drifting overhead.

The three-hour ride begins along the same route as the one-hour trip, but continues up the valley to the Harmony Borax Works. After tying up their horses, they take a 30-minute self-guided walking tour of the site. On the tour, they pass the remains of the refinery and outlying buildings, used from 1882 to 1889 for the processing of borax.

Nearby stands one of the famous 20-Mule-Team wagons that carried borax 165 miles through the desert to Mojave. The ruins of additional buildings can be seen only a short distance away. After completing the tour, riders remount and ride back through the salt flats to the stables.

The most interesting rides at Furnace Creek Stables, however, may be the moonlight trips, offered during the week of the full moon each month. Following the same route used for the one-hour trip, riders travel through barren desert countryside by the light of the moon. The unusual lighting effects and curious shadows bring out the haunting beauty of this hostile landscape.

Rates

The one-hour ride is $15. The two-hour ride is $25 and the three-hour ride is $45. The moonlight ride is $20. Private rides are also available for $25 an hour with a two-hour minimum.

Payment Method

Furnace Creek Stables accepts cash, personal checks, and traveler's checks.

Rider Age Limit

Riders must be at least six years old. On the moonlight ride, the age limit is 12 years old.

How To Get There

From Highway 15 in Baker, take Highway 127 north. At Death Valley Junction, take Highway 190 west. Turn off at Furnace Creek Ranch. Follow the road through the parking lot of Furnace Creek Ranch to the end.

The Rankin Ranch main residence

The old Rankin Ranch barn once used as a stagecoach stop

SOUTHERN MOUNTAINS AND DESERT 11

QUARTER CIRCLE U RANKIN RANCH

P.O. Box 36
Caliente, California 93518
(805) 867-2526
Owner: Helen Rankin

In 1863, a young man named Walker Rankin moved to California and started a cattle ranch in the Tehachapi Mountains. Fresh from Pennsylvania, the youthful Rankin decided to introduce a new breed of cattle, the White Face (Hereford), to the region.

More than a century later, the Rankin family continues to raise White Face cattle on their 31,000-acre ranch located in northeastern Kern County. Today, the Quarter Circle U Rankin Ranch has also become one of the most popular guest ranches in California.

For city-weary vacationers, it's a wonderful escape. Located at 3,500 feet elevation, the ranch offers fresh air, open skies, and plenty of warm hospitality. The accommodations are comfortable and there is plenty for all members of the family to do.

The most popular activity, of course, is horseback riding. Every morning and afternoon, except on Sundays, wranglers lead one-hour trail rides out across the vast acreage of the ranch.

At the higher elevations, up among the pines, riders have a splendid view of Walker's Basin. Along these mountain trails, they can sometimes see deer darting about.

Riders can expect to see carpets of wildflowers in the meadows during the springtime and trees full of color on the mountainsides in the fall.

For the most part, the horses stick to a walk during the trail rides, with an occasional trot. Sometimes, however, when the terrain permits, riders can even break into a gentle lope.

Other Activities

When guests are not busy riding the trails, they can relax by the heated swimming pool or play a few sets of tennis. They can also try their hand at archery, ping pong, volleyball, pool, or horseshoes. Down at

Julia Lake, they can fish for rainbow trout, which the staff will happily cook up for the guest's breakfast.

The Quarter Circle U provides games, crafts, and a talent show for the kids. They also conduct hay rides, barbecues, and cookouts that the whole family will enjoy.

Accommodations

The main ranch house has an interesting history. It was originally built in the early 1870s from a plan published in *Godey's Ladies Book.* All the nails were hand-forged at the ranch and all the lumber was cut up on Breckenridge Mountain. Today, it is filled with antique furniture and family heirlooms.

The wood-paneled rooms are not plush, but they're homey and comfortable. Each comes with a connecting private bath and all feature large picture windows that provide a view of the mountains nearby.

Two adults in one room are $110 per person. The off-season rate for two adults ranges from $85 to $95, depending upon time of week. Single adults are $120. The off-season rate for singles range from $95 to $105. A third and forth adult in a room is $90 for each. The off-season rates for the additional occupants range from $75 to $85.

Children under 12 in a room with their parents are $70 each. The off-season rate for children range from $50 to $60. Children in a room by themselves pay the full adult rate. Guests who stay a week receive a five percent discount.

The Quarter Circle U Rankin Ranch operates on the American Plan, with all meals and activities included in the basic rate.

Dining

The rich history of the ranch is on display in the dining room as guests gather at mealtimes. The walls are covered with old photographs and the tables are set with the family's antique china and silver.

Lunch and dinner are served buffet style, with typical entrees at dinner including, roast, pork chops, chicken, ham, barbecued ribs, and tri-tips. Typical luncheon items include hamburgers, hot dogs, spaghetti, tamale pie, and sandwiches.

Breakfast might feature pancakes, waffles or eggs.

Horse Rental Rates

All horseback riding is included in the basic charge for accommodations.

Payment Method

The Quarter Circle U Rankin Ranch accepts cash, personal checks, traveler's checks, Visa, and MasterCard.

Rider Age Limit

Riders must be at least four years old. However, young riders are restricted to the corral until they are experienced enough to go out on the trail.

Nearest Airport

The closet commercial airport is located in Bakersfield.

How To Get There

From Highway 58, take the Caliente turn off. Continue along the road going east. Three miles past Caliente, the road forks. Take the left fork to the Quarter Circle U Rankin Ranch.

MAGIC MOUNTAIN STABLES

40355 Big Bear Boulevard
Big Bear Lake, California 92315
(714) 866-7715
Owner: Dave Hart

There is much about Big Bear Lake that has changed since it was first discovered and named back in 1845 by Benjamin D. Wilson, a rancher from San Bernardino. Not only are the grizzly bears that inspired the lake's name long gone, but the lake itself has grown in size. After the construction of the Bear Valley Dam in 1884, the lake grew to seven miles in length.

Magic Mountain Stables, located near the lake, offer 45-minute and two-hour trail rides that go up into the national forest. Open 9:00 a.m. to 4:30 p.m. in the summer and 10:00 a.m. to 4:30 p.m. in the winter, Magic Mountain Stables operate without a set time table. The policy for the 45-minute ride is first come, first served. Vacationers must reserve the two-hour ride in advance.

Both trips take off along the same trail. Known to old-timers as the Red Ant Trail, it winds up into a forest of Jeffrey pine, black oak, and white fir in an area to the west of the lake.

On the 45-minute ride, the trail makes what is essentially a loop. The pace of the 45-minute ride is slow. Riders frequently double up with small children, so no running is permitted. Along the way, riders cross a gurgling mountain stream.

The biggest photo opportunity of the 45-minute trip, however, comes when the trail opens up on a view of Big Bear Lake and the whole Big Bear Valley down below. After taking in the view, riders head on back to the stables.

Riders can enjoy views of the lake on the two-hour trip as well. They then proceed on up to a ridge that separates the Big Bear Valley from the Santa Ana River canyon on the other side. Along the ridge, riders come to a spot called the Grand View Point. Looking off to the east, they can see the dramatic mountain peaks of the San Gorgonio Wilderness, which during the winter and spring are covered with snow. From the ridge, they return back down through the thick forest to the stables.

One of the interesting features of Magic Mountain Stables is that they are open all year. In the wintertime, vacationers can go for a ride through a Currier and Ives wonderland of snow. Of course, riders need to give some consideration to the weather and should dress appropriately. With the stables located at close to 6,800 feet elevation, riders can expect to see plenty of snow.

Rates

The 45-minute ride is $20 and the two-hour ride is $40. There is also a $5 charge, when children double up on a horse with a parent.

Payment Method

Magic Mountain Stables accepts cash and traveler's checks only.

Rider Age Limit

Riders must be at least seven years old to ride alone. Children ages two through six may double with a parent.

How To Get There

From Big Bear City, take Big Bear Boulevard west towards the dam. Look for Magic Mountain Stables on the left.

SMOKE TREE STABLES

2500 Toledo Avenue
Palm Springs, California 92264
(619) 327-1372
Owner: Rod Johnson

Just south of the city's lively center, nestled amid the lush green lawns and elegant red-tiled homes of the Canyon Estates area, sits Smoke Tree Stables. Nearby, is the magnificent Andreas Canyon on the Agua Caliente Indian Reservation.

Four times a day–8:00 a.m., 10:00 a.m., 2:00 p.m., and 4:00 p.m.–Smoke Tree Stables offers escorted tours up into the canyon. The trips, which last two hours, give riders a chance to visit an area that is home to the second largest collection of palm trees (*Washingtonia filifera*) in the world.

During the ride through the Reservation, there is enough of an elevation gain that riders are afforded some breathtaking views of the entire Palm Springs region. Along the way, they encounter dramatic rock formations containing Cahuilla rock art, a mountain stream, and 150 different species of plants.

For riders preferring a shorter excursion, Smoke Tree Stables also offers ten one-hour trips a day. They leave every hour on the hour from 8:00 a.m. to 5:00 p.m. Riders go along a nearby wash and through some undeveloped portions of the surrounding residential neighborhood.

Limited though the one-hour trip is, it does offer excellent panoramas of Mount San Jacinto, which looms off to the west. There is little else about this ride, however, that makes it worth recommending. Unless vacationers are looking for nothing more than a chance to ride on a horse, they should select the two-hour ride.

There's one additional recommendation. Avoid riding in the desert during the summer. Smoke Tree Stables limits its summer schedule to early morning rides because of the intense heat. It sometimes closes altogether during July and August.

Rates

The basic charge for rides at Smoke Tree Stables is $18 per hour. There is an additional $3.50 added to the rate for the two-hour ride to cover the admission fee to the Agua Caliente Indian Reservation. The total for the two-hour ride is $39.50. Children may double with a parent for $5.

Payment Method

Smoke Tree Stables accepts cash, personal checks with I.D., and traveler's checks.

Rider Age Limit

Riders must be at least five years old. Children one-and-a-half to five may double with a parent.

How To Get There

From Interstate 10, turn right on Highway 111, which becomes Palm Canyon Drive. Proceed south on Palm Canyon Drive through the center of town. Eventually, the street becomes East Palm Canyon Drive. Turn right on Sunrise Way. Then turn left on Toledo Avenue. Smoke Tree Stables is at the end of the block on the left.

IVEY RANCH EQUESTRIAN CENTER

75-205 Shadow Valley Road
Palm Desert, California 92260
(619) 345-3771
Owner: John B. Ivey, Jr.

Just a short distance from the luxurious estates of Rancho Mirage, vacationers will discover the Coachella Valley Preserve. It's a 13,000 acre nature sanctuary for the rare fringe-toed lizard that has successfully managed to keep developers at bay.

John Ivey, owner of the Ivey Ranch Equestrian Center

Twice each day, the Ivey Ranch Equestrian Center offers a two-hour trail ride that goes right through the Coachella Valley Preserve. The rides, which are by reservation only, start at 8:30 a.m. and 1:30 p.m. throughout most of the year. During the hot summer months, the rides begin at 7:00 a.m. and 6:00 p.m.

The two-hour trip takes riders out across the open desert to Willis Palms, a small oasis in the eastern foothills. As riders head out, they can see the stark beauty of the barren Little San Bernardino Mountains off in the distance. The more immediate surroundings are predominantly sandy with creosote plants dotting the landscape.

Upon reaching Willis Palms, riders get a chance to see the infamous San Andreas Fault up close. From there, the trail heads up a ridge that offers a scenic view of the entire Palm Springs area. Riders then head back west along the same trail.

For riders looking for a more extended desert experience, the Ivey Ranch Equestrian Center also arranges private overnight trips.

There is one thing, however, to keep in mind about riding through the Coachella Valley Preserve. Almost the entire trip takes place out in the open, under the sun. Therefore, it's recommended that riders bring along a canteen. It's also recommended that this trip, like all trips in the desert, be avoided altogether during the summer.

Rates

The charge for the standard two-hour ride is $25. Call or write the Ivey Ranch Equestrian Center to obtain the rates for the longer trips.

Payment Method

Ivey Ranch Equestrian Center accepts only cash and traveler's checks.

Rider Age Limit

Riders must be at least 12 years old.

How To Get There

From Interstate 10, exit at Monterey Avenue. Turn at Varner Road and proceed south. At Chase School Road, make a left turn and proceed east. Turn right on Shadow Valley Road. Then follow the signs.

RANCH OF THE 7TH RANGE

Avenue 58
La Quinta, California 92253
(619) 564-1414
Owner: J.C. Bryan

For most people, the name La Quinta means one thing – a luxurious resort community with lush, green golf courses and championship tennis courts. Little thought is usually given to the stark, brown range of mountains nearby that serve as an ever-present backdrop.When examined more closely, however, these mountains, the Santa Rosas, take on a life and a beauty all their own.

The area is accessible on foot, of course. But there's an even better way for visitors to get a taste of the desert. The Ranch of the 7th Range, located just behind PGA West in La Quinta, offers guided trail rides that go right up into the Santa Rosas. The rides, offered in small groups according to riding ability, vary in length depending upon the wishes of the riders. Most riders, however, find that one-and-a-half hours is about the right amount of time to see the sights.

The trip begins with riders setting off into the foothills. As all signs of development disappear, the landscape becomes a mixture of sand and rocks dotted with barrel cactus, ocotillo, desert ironwood, and creosote.

The trail then heads up into the mountains. On the one-and-a-half-hour trip, riders gain substantial elevation. Looking back, they have an inspiring view of the Coachella Valley, stretching all the way down to the Salton Sea. At the half-way point, riders begin the rather steep descent back down to the stables, which are located 40 feet below sea level.

On the trail near Idyllwild in the San Jacinto Mountains

The Ranch of the 7th Range is open all year round, but it's closed on Sundays during the summer to give the horses and the wranglers a rest.

There's one more thing. Bring plenty of sun block, because there is no cover along the trail whatsoever.

Additional Facilities

For an entirely different riding experience, the Ranch of the 7th Range has a second riding stable located at the Thousand Trails Resort near the charming mile-high town of Idyllwild. Open from May through November each year, it offers trail rides through the scenic alpine terrain of the San Jacinto Mountains.

For those familiar with the Sierra Nevada, the landscape is quite similar. This isn't too surprising, of course, when you consider that the geological origins of the two mountain ranges are so much alike. It's an area of thick pine and cedar forests, large granite outcroppings, and sparkling mountain streams.

Geared to families, the stable offers half-hour and hour trail rides as well as overnight trips for the more ambitious. Call the main office in La Quinta for more information.

Rates

Guided trail rides are $25 per hour.

Payment Method

The Ranch of the 7th Range accepts only cash, personal checks, and traveler's checks.

Rider Age Limit

There is no age limit. Smaller children may double with parents or ride a pony with a lead line.

How To Get There

From Interstate 10 near Indio, exit at Jefferson Avenue. Follow Jefferson west to Avenue 58. Turn right on Avenue 58 and head into La Quinta. Look for the Ranch of the 7th Range on the left. The back of PGA West will be on the right.

To reach the facility near Idyllwild, take Highway 234 south from Interstate 10 at Banning. Continue up into the mountains until you reach Pine Cove. Turn left at the Pine Cove Fire Station and follow the signs up the road to Thousand Trails Resort. At the guard gate, tell the guard that you are going to the Ranch of the 7th Range. The guard will provide a map that takes you right there.

The beach at Malibu

SOUTH COAST 12

RED BARN STABLES

Mullholland Highway
Malibu, CA 90265
(818) 707-9395
Owner: Ted Johnson

There are few stretches of coastline in all of California more fabled or fantasized about than the fashionable enclave along Malibu Beach. The bronzed, the buff, and the briefly-attired can regularly be found frolicking in the Malibu sand, while ensconced nearby in spacious beach-front homes are the incredibly rich and the unbelievably famous. Everyone, it seems, from Bob Dylan to Goldie Hawn lives within a frisbee throw of the pounding surf.

It's a great place for the usual seashore activities, of course, and it's a particularly appealing spot for riding a horse. Normally, however, anyone wishing to ride along the beach in this private neighborhood would need their own horse and a few well-connected friends.

But one day every month, Red Barn Stables, located in the hills above Malibu, brings several horses down to a private beach and makes them available for one-hour rides. The date and the location change every month and advance reservations are required. This little inconvenience aside, it's a rare opportunity to go loping along an exclusive beach and even into the surf. Available riding times are limited, however, so reserve early.

During the rest of the month, there are many additional horseback riding opportunities in the hills above Malibu. Red Barn Stables, affiliated with Calamigos Ranch, offers everything from one-hour trail rides to overnight trips that travel through the heart of the Santa Monica Mountains.

The easiest of these is the one-hour ride, which is geared to inexperienced riders. It begins with riders heading out the front driveway onto the shoulder of Mullholland Highway. (It's only called Mullholland Drive within the city limits.) They travel down the road a short distance before crossing over into the entrance of Rocky Oaks Park.

Before 1978, it had been a working cattle ranch, but a savage fire destroyed all the ranch buildings and eventually the National Park Service took over control. Riders travel through the parking lot and into a picnic area, shaded by rangy old oak trees.

Soon they emerge from the trees and follow a trail through the grass up along a small pond, where coots can be seen scurrying by. Rising up behind the pond is an interesting rock outcropping called rather unimaginatively "Hill 1850+." They continue out to the edge of the 197.8-acre property, where they catch a brief view of Agoura down below.

The loop trail begins to rise slightly as riders go past a chaparral-covered slope above the pond. They wind around behind Hill 1850+ and then down and out to Mullholland Highway for the short ride back to the stables.

The two-hour ride is a bit more challenging and affords riders a spectacular view. This popular trip begins with riders turning up Mullholland Highway and following it for several minutes. At a Y in the road near Saddle Rock Ranch, riders veer off to the right. A short distance past the Y, they turn off onto a dirt road that takes them onto the ranch property.

Once off the highway, they ride through rugged countryside before making a steep climb up to the highest point in the surrounding area, a 2,236 foot high bluff. Riders dismount, stretch their legs, and enjoy the wonderful 360-degree view. On a clear day, they're able to see the Channel Islands and Santa Catalina Island off in the distance. Looking inland, they have a bird's eye view of Westlake Village and Agoura.

After climbing back into the saddle, they make a relatively steep descent down into a wide-open field, where they have a chance to run their horses a bit. From the field, they wind back to Mullholland for the ride back to the stables.

There are also three special versions of the ride to the bluff. Five days each month, Red Barn Stables offers a full-moon ride that departs at 9:00 p.m. Following the same route as the regular two-hour trip, riders travel out to the bluff by the light of the moon.

Another special event is the sunset ride. Departing at 4:00 p.m. in the winter and 7:00 p.m. in the summer, riders reach the bluff in time to enjoy the sunset over the Pacific Ocean.

Red Barn Stables also offers a dinner ride. After traveling out to the bluff and back, riders sit down for a hearty meal catered by the Calamigos Ranch. A typical menu includes barbecued chicken, corn on the cob, and chili. Riders must bring along their own beverage and dessert.

For riders looking for more time in the saddle, Red Barn Stables offers a half-day ride. Following the Backbone Trail part of the way, they travel down into the Newton Canyon area and out near 2,528 foot high Castro Peak before completing a loop back. At certain points along the trail, they have excellent ocean views.

The best way for riders to experience the varied terrain, plant life, and scenery in the Santa Monica Mountains, however, is on the all-day ride. Heading down from the stables on Mullholland, riders swing past antenna-topped Castro Peak and then continue on along the Castro

Mountainway to a point where it intersects with the Bulldog Mountainway.

Traveling along the Bulldog Mountainway, riders drop down into what many consider the most beautiful area in the Santa Monica Mountains, Malibu Creek State Park. Once in the park, they encounter a familiar sight. Rising up before them are the dramatic and picturesque Goat Buttes, the towers of craggy rock that appear in the opening title sequence on the television program *M*A*S*H.*

As it happens, Malibu Creek State Park, not Korea, is the real home of the 4077 medical group. It also served as the setting for parts of *How Green Was My Valley, The Swiss Family Robinson,* and *Love Is A Many Splendored Thing.*

The park, only minutes from the clogged freeways, endless shopping strips, and sprawling housing tracts of greater Los Angeles, is remarkably peaceful and serene. As riders move past the sturdy oaks that dot the grassy hillside a lone hawk can often be seen quietly floating overhead. Nearby Malibu Creek makes the only sound. It's a perfect place for lunch. Eventually, riders head back up Bulldog Mountainway on their return to the stables.

For some riders, however, even a day trip is not enough. Fortunately, Red Barn Stables also arranges all-inclusive overnight trips. It's up to the rider to select the destination. Red Barn does the rest. The only real limitation is the availability of camping permits at the selected destination. Point Mugu State Park, for instance, is a very popular choice. Unfortunately, camping permits at Point Mugu must be obtained long in advance.

Rates

The one-hour rides along Malibu Beach are $40. The one-hour trail ride is $20. The two-hour ride is $40 and the half-day ride is $90. The all-day ride is $180. The sunset ride and the full-moon ride are $40 each. The dinner ride is $52. The all-inclusive overnight trip is $240.

Payment Method

Red Barn Stables accepts cash, personal checks, and traveler's checks.

Rider Age Limit

There is no specific age limit, but all riders must be able to handle a horse.

How To Get There

From Pacific Coast Highway in Malibu, turn on to Kanan Road and head up the hill. Turn left on Mullholland Highway. From Highway 101, take Kanan Road up to Mullholland Highway and turn right.

Go up up Mullholland Highway a short distance and look for Red Barn Stables on the left.

GRIFFITH PARK LIVERY
480 Riverside Drive
Burbank, CA 91506
(818) 840-8401
Owner: Art Gottfried

STABLE J.P. STABLES
914 S. Mariposa Street
Burbank, CA 91506
(818) 843-9890
Owner: Valencia Circle K, Inc.

BAR S STABLES
1850 Riverside Drive
Glendale, CA 91201
(818) 242-8443
Owner: DeWayne Stephens

It's five times larger than New York's Central Park and sits in the very heart of metropolitan Los Angeles. Measuring a massive 4,107 acres and sprawling over the eastern end of the Santa Monica Mountains, Griffith Park is the largest urban park in the United States.

For many people, even those living in Southern California, this may come as a surprise. But the park, a generous gift to the city from Col. Griffith J. Griffith back in 1896, provides a wonderful natural playground for residents in the area.

It also provides more opportunities for horseback riders than are likely to be found in any other big city in the country. Within its boundaries, Griffith Park has 45 miles of trails that were specifically created for horseback riding. Immediately adjacent to the park are four stables that offer horses for rent. One of the four, Sunset Stables, located on the Hollywood side of the park, is described in a separate section. The other three–Griffith Park Livery Stable, J.P. Stables, and Bar S Stables–are all situated within a few blocks of each other near the Los Angeles Equestrian Center.

Open seven days a week, virtually every day of the year except Christmas, all three offer unguided rides, though J.P. Stables will provide a guide for those who desire one. Two of the three also have time limits. Griffith Park Livery Stable has a two-hour riding limit and Bar S Stables a four-hour limit. J. P. Stables, on the other hand, permits unlimited riding.

Departing from any of the stables, riders enter Griffith Park by taking a bridge over the Los Angeles River and traveling through a series of tunnels that pass under the Ventura Freeway. The trail comes out near Travel Town, an outdoor museum in the park where a number of old steam engines and railroad cars are on display.

From Travel Town, riders can reach virtually every landmark and scenic spot within the park. The trails wind up and down through the wild grasses, rangy oaks, and chaparral-covered hillsides. While in the park, riders may walk, trot, or lope gently. However, galloping is prohibited by municipal ordinance. Riders are also prohibited from tying up their horses in the park.

One direction they can head is towards the Los Angeles Zoo and right past the Gene Autry Western Heritage Museum, home of the former singing cowboy's collection of western memorabilia. Not far from the zoo, they can visit Amir's Garden, a private landscaping project initiated by an Iranian immigrant Amir Dialameh as a gift to the city. The many trees and bushes he has planted as well as the benches he has constructed have turned it into a pleasant stopping place for park visitors.

A second garden created by another immigrant to Los Angeles, Dante Orgolini, sits on the slope of Mount Hollywood. Considered one of the most romantic spots in Los Angeles to enjoy a sunset, Dante's View is tucked in among the pines, eucalyptus, and palms.

Continuing on up to the top of 1,625 foot high Mount Hollywood, the highest point in Griffith Park, riders enjoy a panoramic view in almost every direction. On a clear day, they can look out across Hollywood and see all the way to Santa Catalina Island. Off in other directions, they catch views of downtown Los Angeles, the San Fernando Valley, and the San Gabriel Mountains in the distance.

Riders can also travel by the three golf courses located within the park – Harding, Wilson, and Roosevelt – and even up to Griffith Observatory. Another trail takes riders down along the border of Forest Lawn Memorial Park. In all, there are more than enough interesting trails to keep riders going for hours and hours.

For those who would like to experience a ride by moonlight, Griffith Park Livery Stable offers special two-hour guided night rides. The rides, arranged for groups of five or more on Mondays through Thursdays and ten or more on Fridays and Saturdays, head up along the ridgeline of the Santa Monica Mountains. From the trail, perched above the San Fernando Valley, riders have a spectacular view of the thousands of twinkling lights that dot the populous region below.

Rates

Griffith Park Livery Stable charges $13 for one hour, $25 for two. J.P. Stables charges $13 for the first hour and $11 for each additional hour. An $11 deposit is also required. Bar S Stables charges $13 per hour and $12 for each additional hour. A $10 deposit is required.

Payment Methods

The three stables accept only cash and traveler's checks.

Rider Age Limit

Griffith Park Livery Stable requires riders to be 12 years or older. J.P. Stables requires riders to be at least six years old and four feet tall. Bar S Stables requires riders to be at least nine years old with a guardian or at least 13 without a guardian.

How To Get There

From the Ventura Freeway in Burbank, take the Buena Vista exit. Go south to Riverside Drive. To reach J.P. Stables, continue along Riverside Drive to Mariposa. Turn right on Mariposa and drive to the end of the street. The stables is on the left.

To reach Griffith Park Livery Stable continue along Riverside Drive past Mariposa to Main Street. At Main Street, enter the Los Angeles Equestrian Center and follow the road through the parking lot to the left. Continue to the end, where you will find Griffith Park Livery Stable on the right.

For those preferring Bar S Stables, continue along Riverside Drive past Main Street. Look for the stables on the right.

SUNSET RANCH

3400 N. Beachwood
Hollywood, CA 90068
(213) 464-9612
Owner: Stephen J. Smith

There they sit on the side of the hill, worn, faded, yet somehow captivating, those nine famous letters that have spelled fantasy, wonder, and delight for millions around the world–H O L L Y W O O D. Originally, constructed as a temporary promotion for a real estate project in the 20s, the sign has become the most recognizable landmark in America's second largest city.

The sign also serves as a handy point of reference for those looking for an entertaining horseback ride in the Los Angeles area. Because hidden in a small canyon just to the right of the Hollywood sign and above the historic Hollywoodland section of Los Angeles is Sunset Ranch. Here travelers get the rare chance to crawl out of their automobiles, at least briefly, and see a bit of Southern California from tall in the saddle.

Sunset Ranch, open from 9:00 a.m. to 5:00 p.m. seven days a week, offers rental horses for trail rides through nearby Griffith Park. It also provides the only access to the park from the Hollywood side, making certain landmarks and trails in the southern end of the park easier to reach. As an added convenience, riders have an option of riding with or without a guide and may stay out on the trails as long as they wish.

Heading up from Sunset Ranch to the ridge that runs through the park, riders get a bird's-eye view of sprawling Los Angeles spread out below them. Familiar landmarks like the Capitol Records building can be easily spotted. Riders also get an unusual side-angle view of the Hollywood sign.

From the ridge, it's only a short ride around and down to one of the most interesting sights in Griffith Park – Bronson Caves. Located in the Brush Canyon area immediately southeast of the stables, the caves will immediately be recognizable to many television viewers. The area served as the site of the Bat Cave in the *Batman* TV series, for instance, and has provided the backdrop for scenes from other shows including *Star Trek* and *Bonanza.*

Another highlight along one of the nearby trails is Griffith Observatory, where James Dean had his famous fight with a gang in *Rebel Without A Cause.* Of course, riders have all of the 45 miles of trails in Griffith Park at their disposal. They can ride up to the highest point in the park, 1,625 foot high Mount Hollywood. They can travel by the Harding, Wilson, and Roosevelt Golf Courses. Or they ride all the way over to Travel Town, the train exhibit on the Burbank side.

The park is rugged, yet scenic, with hillsides covered with tall grass, tangled chaparral, and dotted with oaks. From its highest point to its lowest, the park has elevation changes of up to 1,300 feet.

The most interesting ride at Sunset Ranch takes place in the evening. Starting at 6:00 p.m., riders are taken on a trip through Griffith Park all the way to Burbank. For dinner, a stop is made at Viva's Restaurant in Burbank, where riders get to dine on hot, spicy Mexican food. The cost of dinner is not included in the basic charge for the ride.

After dinner, riders return by starlight. Along the way, they enjoy the brightly-lit skylines of Burbank and Los Angeles. The ride generally ends about 11:00 p.m. During the course of the evening, riders can expect to spend about three hours actually in the saddle.

The Sunset Ranch night ride is available to individual members of the public only on Friday nights. On all other days of the week, the night rides are reserved for private groups of 15 or more riders. Those interested in the Friday night ride should plan on showing up early, because Sunset Ranch does not accept advance reservations. Frequently, a line starts forming as early as 4:00 p.m.

One thing to consider before planning a ride at Sunset Ranch is the air quality in Los Angeles. If the air quality is quite bad, the views will be greatly restricted. On a clear day, of course, you can see for miles and miles. As a general rule, air quality deteriorates during hot weather, so temperature and time of year are good indicators of potential air quality.

If you were to pick the best time to go for a ride in Griffith Park, it would be right after a rain storm.

Rates

The day rides are $15 an hour. A $10 deposit is required. Night rides are a flat $30. The charge for doubling is $25.

Payment Method

Sunset Ranch accepts cash and traveler's checks only.

Rider Age Limit

There is no set limit, but if riders are too small, they must double with a parent.

How To Get There

From the southbound Hollywood Freeway (101), exit at Gower Street and turn left. Go up to Franklin and turn right. Then turn left on Beechwood and continue for three miles to the end of Beechwood. From the northbound Hollywood Freeway, exit at Gower Street and bear right to Beechwood. Then continue to the end of the street.

CATALINA STABLES

600 Avalon Canyon Road
Avalon, CA 90704
(310) 510-0478
Owner: Bunny Putnam

Fabled in story and song, Santa Catalina, the rugged, mountainous, 21-mile long island off the Southern California coast has been a popular resort playground since the 1920s, particularly among the Hollywood elite. Once entirely owned by the Wrigley family, makers of the chewing gum, Santa Catalina Island remains largely undeveloped even today with most of the land now controlled by the non-profit Santa Catalina Island Conservancy.

For Southern Californians weary of gridlocked freeways and dingy smog, a short boat ride over to Catalina serves as a refreshing escape. Upon arriving, visitors can stroll around the charming Mediteranean-style village of Avalon. They can rent motorized golf carts and go scooting around the nearby hills. Or they can take one of the guided bus tours that go into the interior of the island.

Of course, for serious trail riders, there's an even better choice. Catalina Stables, open all year round, offers rides into the hills above the golf course and beyond.

Santa Catalina Island

The easiest of these and the one recommended for inexperienced riders is the one-hour trip. It travels at a slow pace and makes only modest elevation gains, yet it provides a pleasant riding experience and excellent views.

Beginning at the stables, located next to the golf course, riders head up Avalon Canyon Road, sticking to the shoulder. Off to the left, as they continue along the road, are the neatly-trimmed fairways of the nine-hole Catalina Island Golf Course, the oldest in Southern California. Further up the palm-tree lined road, riders pass Bird Park, an aviary created by William Wrigley, Jr many years ago.

Continuing past Joe Machado Memorial Ball Park, they turn off onto a dirt trail that heads up into the chaparal-covered hills. Known as the Lower Trail, it winds around behind the golf course, providing splendid views of the picturesque Casino and scenic Avalon Bay down below.

Eventually, riders work their way back down to the golf course, where they cross in front of one of the tees on their way back to the corral.

Catalina Stables also offers a one-and-a-half-hour ride that covers much of the same territory, while adding an extra trail to the loop that takes riders higher up into the hills. Intended for more experienced riders, the longer trip provides even better views of Avalon Bay and the surrounding community.

The most interesting trip, however, is the five-hour ride, available only for experienced riders by advanced arrangement. Beginning along the same route used for the other two trips, riders continue on up Avalon Canyon Road to Hermit Gulch Campground. At this point, they venture off onto a trail that climbs right up into the mountains. It's a tough ride along a narrow trail as they climb up to the ridgeline. But the view is spectacular. On a clear day, they can see all the way to the mainland.

Going past the microwave tower that sits on top of the ridge, they continue on to Haypress Reservoir, looking for wildlife along the way. In addition to wild boar, Channel Island foxes, goats, and deer, Santa Catalina Island is home to a herd of buffalo. Originally brought over in 1924 for the movie *The Vanishing American,* a group of 14 buffalo has since grown to a herd numbering roughly 200 head.

At Haypress Reservoir, riders stop for lunch and a chance to stretch their legs, before returning back along the same trail they took out. As they return to the stables, they have one last chance to enjoy an eagle's eye view of the island from the top of the ridge.

Rates

The one-hour ride is $25. The hour-and-a-half ride is $30 on weekdays and $35 on weekends and holidays. The five-hour ride is $100 and is available by advance arrangement only. Reservations for the other two rides must be made in person. There is a sign at the stables that says, "If you enjoyed your ride, pet your horse and tip your guide."

Payment Method

Catalina Stables accepts only cash and traveler's checks.

Rider Age Limit

All riders must be at least eight years old and children must have had previous riding experience.

How To Get There

Boat service to Santa Catalina Island is available from San Pedro, Long Beach, Newport Beach, and San Diego. Air transportation is also available. Once on the island, take Avalon Canyon Road from downtown Avalon. Look for the sign for Catalina Stables on the left side of the road near the golf course.

SYCAMORE TRAILS STABLES

26282 Oso Road
San Juan Capistrano, CA 92675
(714) 661-1755
Owner: Ron Hanson

When Richard Henry Dana, author of *Two Years Before The Mast,* wrote about San Juan Capistrano after his visit in 1834, he never even mentioned the fabled swallows. By then, of course, the phenomena of their annual return had already been observed for more than a half century. But in those days, other things were more important in that region – specifically, cattle ranching for the cowhide trade.

Not that the swallows are unimportant. Their uncanny timing and unerring sense of direction continue to fascinate. But there simply is more to the history of the region than the comings and goings of those indefatigable swallows. Cows and horses have played an important role in the life of San Juan Capistrano, as well.

These days, there isn't much ranch land left, of course. Orange groves and ultimately subdivisions have seen to that. Fortunately, there's still one place, where it's possible to ride a horse where the vaqueros once roamed. Sycamore Trails Stables, located roughly a mile from the mission, offers one-hour trail rides through one of the last undeveloped areas in San Juan Capistrano.

Open seven days a week, the stables schedules rides at 8:30 a.m., 10:00 a.m., 11:30 a.m., 1:30 p.m., 3:00 p.m., 4:30 p.m., and 5.45 p.m. All the trips, which are guided, follow the same basic route and include cantering along certain stretches.

From the stables, riders head off along a trail that follows Oso Creek as it winds up through the willows. Recent discoveries of artifacts along the creek suggest that this was once an area where Native Americans settled. After some distance, riders pass through an abandoned orange grove, one of the few in Orange County that have been left to die naturally rather than at the hand of developers.

From the grove, riders begin to climb part way up one of the rolling hills that are so typical of this region. Depending upon the time of year, these hills are either covered with lush, green wild grass or a drier, browner version of the same thing. From a point half way up, they swing around and follow a road heading south. As they continue, riders pass the occasional rangy, old oak tree and a stand of eucalyptus down below.

It's along this stretch that they have the best view. Looking around they have a panoramic view of the Saddleback Valley. These days, of course, that means having a sweeping view of a major interstate highway and endless housing projects. But there are still hints of the natural beauty of the region that once existed before red tile roofs started spreading like some inoperable disease.

Closer at hand, riders can look down on the roofs of some of the mission buildings poking through the trees. Twice each day, they can even hear the bells of the mission summoning the faithful to pray. They continue to follow the trail as it swings west and then drops back down into a second abandoned orange grove. Eventually, the trail winds back to the stable.

Clearly, Sycamore Trails Stables does not offer the variety of rides or the range of scenery found elsewhere. But it is a well-run operation and riders do get to do some loping. That alone should insure that they'll have an enjoyable riding experience.

Rates

The charge for the one-hour ride is $20.

Payment Methods

Sycamore Trails Stables accepts cash, personal checks, traveler's checks, Visa, and MasterCard.

Rider Age Limit

Riders must be at least seven years old.

How To Get There

From Interstate 5, take the Junipero Serra exit. Turn left on Camino Capistrano and proceed to Oso. Turn right on Oso Road, go over the railroad tracks and turn left at the first opportunity after crossing the tracks. Sycamore Trails Stables is at the end of the road.

HOLIDAYS ON HORSEBACK

24928 Viejas Blvd.
Descanso, CA 91916
(619) 445-3997
Owners: Earl and Elizabeth Hammond

For 7,000 years, it was the private mountain paradise of the Kumeya'ay Indians. Only an invasion of gold prospectors in the 1870s finally drove them off the land they called Ah-ha-Kwe-ah-mac–"the place where it rains."

Today, thanks to good fortune and the generous action of one civic-minded citizen, the area has become a state park and its natural beauty is available for all to enjoy. Cuyamaca Rancho State Park, located halfway between the coastline and the desert, is one of the true gems in all of Southern California, containing over 25,000 acres to take in. Fortunately for trail riders, there's also a great way to explore it.

Holidays on Horseback, located in nearby Descanso, offers a number of interesting trail rides that go in and around Cuyamaca Rancho State Park. What makes these rides particularly appealing is that they use some of the most impressive horses around – Missouri Foxtrotters, Tennessee Walkers, Peruvian Passos, and Paso Finos.

In all of California, Holidays on Horseback is the only rental stable that uses gaited horses for trail rides. That makes it a rare find, because a gaited horse provides an unusually smooth ride. Often, for instance, a trot on a gaited horse is less bumpy than a walk on any other horse.

The southern end of Cuyamaca Rancho State Park

It's the perfect combination, a smooth ride and attractive scenery. How much of the scenery riders get to see, however, depends on the length of the ride. The shortest trip, the two-hour ride only loops through a lower portion of the park. The three-hour trip, which comes with either a snack or a full barbecue dinner, makes a higher loop.

The five-hour, seven-hour, and nine-hour trips, which include lunch, cover even more territory. On the nine-hour trip, in fact, riders travel all the way to Lake Cuyamaca at the north end of the park and back.

Even on the shorter trips, however, riders have an opportunity to discover at least part of the wide variety of vegetation that grows there. Within the park's boundaries, riders can travel through forests containing everything from Coulter, sugar, ponderosa, and Jeffrey pine to white fir, incense cedar, willow, alder, sycamore, and canyon live oak. They can also travel through spacious meadows, past chaparral-covered hillsides, and across a number of meandering creeks and streams.

Along the trail, they can encounter any number of four-legged creatures, including badgers, bobcats, coyotes, deer, raccoons, and mountain lions. In addition, they have an opportunity to spot some of the over 100 different species of birds that frequent the region.

Cuyamaca Rancho State Park is also a place where riders can experience the changing of the seasons. Wild flowers burst out in the springtime, the deciduous trees change colors in the fall, and there are times in the winter when the park even gets coated with snow.

For those who are attracted by the setting, but would prefer to go at a faster pace, Holidays on Horseback offers "boogie" rides for groups of from three to four experienced riders. As the name suggests, it's an opportunity to go at a full-tilt boogie and promises all who participate a rip-roaring good time.

Special Programs

Probably the most interesting and unusual activity offered by Holidays on Horseback, however, is its three-day Mountain Man Ride, a combination trail ride, wilderness survival course, and backwoods history lesson. For many participants, it has the same profound effect on them that cattle drives and other intense outdoor experiences have on people more accustomed to the work-a-day world of the city.

The originator of the Mountain Man Ride and its principal instructor is Earl Hammond, owner of Holidays on Horseback. Once the trainer of the Kodiak bear that appeared in a long-running series of Hamm's Beer commercials, Earl brings a lifetime of wilderness experience to what is clearly a labor of love. During the three days, he spends a good deal of time sharing what he has learned.

The trip begins with an all-day ride through varied wilderness terrain to a camp site on the shores of a private lake. Upon arrival, Earl and the participants, who generally number between ten and twelve, begin setting up the hand-made tepees that provide shelter during the stay. At dinner time, the group gathers for a meal of buffalo stew that's cooked over a fire started with flint and steel. Then after listening to Earl regale them with tales of the history and romance of this part of the world, everyone crawls off to sleep on a bed of pine needles.

The following morning, the group eats a hearty breakfast and then hits the trail for a two to three hour ride. The balance of the day is spent learning valuable survival skills like finding your direction when lost, identifying edible plants, tracking animals, and locating natural sources of medicine. Earl even demonstrates toolmaking as he creates a primitive tomahawk from scratch.

On the final day, the group rides back to the stable, stopping for lunch at a spot inside Cuyamaca Rancho State Park that was once used by the Kumeya'ay Indians; grinding holes used for making paste out of acorns can be seen in the nearby rocks. Though it's only a three-day experience, it's one most participants never forget.

For vacationers interested in a more conventional overnight trail ride experience, those are available as well. Among the more interesting are trips to the Anza-Borrego Desert. During these visits, riders have an opportunity to observe wild mustangs and mountain sheep and to experience one of the most scenic desert environments in California. Generally, of course, these trips are conducted during the cooler times of the year.

Holidays on Horseback offers one other unique program – van tours around the back country of San Diego. Included in the all-day tours are lunch, an hour-and-a-half trail ride, and a visit to either the historic town of Julian or Anza-Borrego Desert State Park. Vacationers can arrange to be picked up for these tours at hotels and motels around San Diego.

Additional Facilities

Holidays on Horseback also offers trail rides out of the Rancho Penasquitos Equestrian Center, which sits across the street from the east end of the seven-mile long Los Penasquitos Canyon Preserve. It provides an excellent way to explore the unique canyon that contains 2,500 acres of trees, grasslands, historical relics, a lazy creek, and even a small waterfall. Though surrounded by housing developments, its sheer size and ample vegetation manage to preserve much of its park-like feeling.

Rates

The two-hour ride is $30. The three-hour ride with a snack and beverage is $45 and with a full barbecue dinner is $60. The four-hour ride with lunch is $55. The five-hour ride with lunch is $70 per person for groups up to six and $65 per person for larger groups. The seven-hour ride with lunch is $100 per person for groups up to six and $90 per person for larger groups. The nine-hour ride with lunch is $125 per person for groups up to six and $100 per person for larger groups.

Two-day camping rides are $350. Three-day camping rides are $525 and four-day camping rides are $700. These rates for camping rides also apply to the Mountain Man Ride.

All-day van tours to Julian are $99. Tours to Anza-Borrego Desert State Park are $125. Both trips include lunch and a trail ride.

The one-hour ride at Los Penasquitos Canyon Preserve is $15. The two-hour ride is $30. The three-hour ride with snack is $45 and the four-hour ride with lunch is $60.

Payment Method

Holidays on Horseback accepts cash, personal checks, traveler's checks, Visa, MasterCard, and Discover.

Rider Age Limit

All riders must be at least five years old.

How To Get There

Take Interstate 8 east from San Diego. Exit at Highway 79/Julian offramp. At the stop sign, go left on Highway 79. Proceed to Riverside Drive. The Descanso Station Restaurant will be on the left. Turn left on Riverside Drive and proceed to Perkins Store, staying to the right at the fork. Follow Viejas Blvd., bearing right at the curve. Turn left on Mizpah Lane and look for the sign.

To reach Rancho Penasquitos Equestrian Center, take Highway 15 north towards Poway. Exit at Mercy Road and proceed to Black Mountain Road. Look for the sign near the intersection of Mercy Road and Black Mountain Road.

BRIGHT VALLEY FARM

11990 Campo Road
Spring Valley, CA 91977
(619) 670-1861
Owners: Marge, Tamara, and Michael Armour

Maybe it's the almost-perfect weather. Or perhaps it's the gentle, rolling hills. But, whatever the reason, San Diego County has always been a great place to raise horses. Sadly, however, that seems to be changing. San Diego's once-plentiful pasturelands are fast giving way to housing developments.

That's why discovering a large horse ranch nestled in the San Diego suburbs is such a pleasant surprise. Somehow, Bright Valley Farm, a 350-acre spread in the Spring Valley area has managed to survive the onslaught of red tile and stucco.

For vacationers, this means there is still a place close to the city where they can go for an enjoyable ride on a quality horse. There is plenty of room on the ranch to do some serious riding and the horses themselves are outstanding.

Unlike most rental stables, Bright Valley Farm breeds and raises most of its own stock, which includes Quarter horses, Arabians, and Appaloosas. The ranch is also one of the few in the state that allows riders to choose either an English or a Western saddle.

During the escorted rides, available Tuesday through Sunday, riders travel along the tree-lined Sweetwater River, home to a variety of interesting water fowl. Then they head up into the chaparral-covered foothills above, where they have a wide view of the surrounding valley.

Coyote and deer have been known to roam these foothills and red-tail hawks are a fairly common sight. In addition, relics of the area's rich and colorful past dot the hillside. Sharp-eyed riders may, for instance, spot grindstones left by the Indians who once lived in this coastal valley. Riders can also go past the remains of a stone building erected by the Butterfield Stage Line, back when it serviced the region. Its roof has collapsed, but the walls are still standing.

The next generation at Bright Valley Farm

The length and route of each trip depends primarily on the experience and expressed interest of the riders. More experienced riders will be happy to know that loping is permitted.

Aside from its regular trail rides, Bright Valley Farm also offers a special full-moon ride once each month. Normally, it is scheduled on the Saturday closest to the full moon at 7:00 p.m. The event, however, is intended for more advanced riders only.

Rates

The standard rate is $12.50 per hour. The full-moon ride is $20.

Payment Method

Bright Valley Farm accepts cash, personal checks, and traveler's checks.

Rider Age Limit

All riders must be at least seven years old.

How To Get There

From Interstate 5 near San Diego, take Highway 94 east. At Campo Road, turn right. Campo Road is unmarked, so look for the Union 76 gas station on the left at the stop light. Proceed down Campo Road and watch for the sign on the left.

HILLTOP STABLE

2671 Monument
San Diego, CA 92154
(619) 428-5441
Owner: Wanda Moore

SANDI'S RENTAL STABLE

2060 Hollister
San Diego, CA 92154
(619) 424-3124
Owner: Ron Mullis

There is a great deal of history associated with the border between the United States and Mexico. Its creation in 1848 by the Treaty of Guadalupe Hildalgo ended Mexico's once dominate control over Alta California and established a clear boundary.

But as visitors to Border Field State Park in southern San Diego County soon discover, the historical events that created the border are really more interesting than the border area itself. Admittedly, the sight of Tijuana's Bullring-by-the-Sea only yards from the park boundary is a surprise. Even the on-going cat and mouse game between the border patrol and suspected visa violators is worth a second glance. But neither the bullring nor the border patrol are enough to justify a visit.

There is one thing about Border Field State Park, however, that makes it enormously appealing, at least to trail riders. The park happens to contain the one beach in San Diego County on which people can ride a horse and there are few places anywhere that offer riding that's more wide open.

Fortunately, finding a horse isn't difficult, either. There are two stables near the park – Hilltop Stable and Sandi's Rental Stable – that offer horses for hire by the hour.

Hilltop Stable is the more professional operation and clearly has the better quality horses. However, the only way that riders can reach the beach from Hilltop Stable is along the shoulder of Monument Road, a 45-minute trip. Riding along the road isn't particularly dangerous, but it's hardly ideal. Border patrol cars come whizzing by on a fairly regular basis. If that's not a concern, however, Hilltop Stable might be the preferable choice.

Sandi's Stable is less impressive than its neighbor, but it does have one appealing feature. The route from Sandi's to the beach goes along the road for only the first 15 minutes. After that, riders travel through a nature preserve that's home to over 340 different species of birds. They also cross the Tijuana River, before completing their 45-minute ride to the beach.

The surf at Border Field State Park

Both stables provide guides part way out, but then riders are on their own. Once at the beach, they can take their horses into the water, canter across the all-but-deserted sand, or head down to the border to catch a glimpse of the Tijuana coastline. Actually crossing the border, however, is strongly discouraged. The beach, though not fenced off, is not considered a legal crossing point and venturing over into Tijuana could create unnecessary hassels.

Instead, riders might take their horses down to the spot where the border meets the tide, allowing them to stand on the southwestern most point in the continental United States. As trivia buffs know, there are only three other comparable places in the country–in Key Largo, Florida; Madawaska, Maine; and Cape Flattery, Washington.

After they've finished riding along the beach, riders return along the same route they started from.

Rates

The standard rate at both stables is $15 per hour. When riders rent for two hours, the third hour is free.

Payment Method

Only cash and travelers checks are accepted at either place.

Rider Age Limit

Children six and over can ride their own horse. Younger children can double with their parents at no charge.

How To Get There

To reach Hilltop Stable, take the Dairy Mart exit from Interstate 5. Proceed south on Dairy Mart Road. Eventually, bear left onto Monument. Go two miles and look for the sign on the left side of the road.

To reach Sandi's Rental Stable, take the Coronado exit from Interstate 5. Go through the stop sign and the road becomes Hollister. Go a mile-and-a-half and look for the sign on the right.

ABOUT THE AUTHOR

Destined from birth to become a cowboy, John A. Greenwald somehow ended up working in the wild and wooly world of advertising instead. Now, rather than rounding up little doggies, he rides herd over wandering metaphors, rampaging double-entendres, and unruly split infinitives, while writing ads for a number of well-known clients.

A native Californian, he grew up on the Monterey Peninsula and graduated from the University of California at Berkeley. Today, he and his wife Carol make their home in Irvine.